leader Daniel O'Connell *(see p16)*, who lived at No. 58 and poet W B Yeats *(see p23)*, who lived at No. 82. Oscar Wilde *(see p23)* spent his childhood at No. 1.

The attractive central park features colourful flower and shrub beds. In the 1840s it served a grim function as an emergency soup kitchen, feeding the hungry during the Great Famine *(see p17)*. On the northwest side of the park stands the restored Rutland Fountain. It was originally erected in 1791 for the sole use of Dublin's poor.

Just off the square, at No. 24 Merrion Street Upper, is the birthplace of the Duke of Wellington, who, when he was teased about his Irish background, famously said, "Being born in a stable does not make one a horse."

The recreated Georgian kitchen of Number 29, Fitzwilliam Street Lower

Royal Hibernian Academy ⑳

15 Ely Place. **Map** E5. **Tel** 661 2558. ◯ *11am–5pm Tue–Wed & Fri–Sat, 11am–8pm Thu, 2–5pm Sun.* ◉ *public hols.* ♿ *limited access.* **www.**royalhibernianacademy.com

The academy is one of the largest exhibition spaces in the city. It puts on exhibitions of Irish and international artists showing both traditional and innovative forms of visual art. This modern brick-and-plate-glass building does, however, look out of place at the end of Ely Place, an attractive Georgian cul-de-sac.

Number 29 ㉑

29 Fitzwilliam St Lower. **Map** F5. **Tel** 702 6165. ◯ *10am–5pm Tue–Sat, 1–5pm Sun.* ◉ *two weeks prior to Christmas.* 📷 ✂ **www.**esb.ie/numbertwentynine

Number 29 is a corner townhouse, built in 1794 for a Mrs Olivia Beattie whose late husband was a wine and paper merchant. While the period furniture comes from the collection of the National Museum, the main purpose of this exhibit is to give visitors a behind-the-scenes look at how middle-class Georgians went about their daily business. Tours start with a short slide show and then work their way through the building from the cellar upwards. Along the way are mahogany tables, chandeliers, Turkish carpets and landscape paintings (by Thomas Roberts among others) but of most interest are some of the quirkier items. Guides point out rudimentary hostess trolleys, water filters and even a Georgian baby walker, as well as an early exercise machine, used to tone up the muscles for horse riding. A tea caddy takes pride of place in one of the reception rooms: at today's prices a kilo of tea would have cost 800 and hence the lady of the house kept the key to the caddy on her person at all times.

The elegant gardens in Merrion Square, a quiet backwater in the centre of Dublin

National Gallery ⑱

This purpose-built gallery was opened to the public in 1864. It houses many excellent exhibits, largely due to generous bequests, such as the Milltown collection of works of art from Russborough House (*see p108*). Playwright George Bernard Shaw was also a benefactor, leaving a third of his estate to the gallery. A new wing has been added to the gallery, which today has more than 500 works on display. Although the emphasis is on Irish art, the major schools of European painting are well represented.

The Houseless Wanderer by John Foley

★ Pierrot
This Cubist-style work, by Spanish-born artist Juan Gris, is one of many variations he painted on the theme of Pierrot and Harlequin. This particular one dates from 1921.

GALLERY GUIDE

The main entrance to the gallery is through the lofty Millennium Wing on Clare Street. Irish and British collections are housed on level 1, as is the National Portrait Gallery. The European schools are located on level 2, with changing special exhibitions installed in the Millennium Wing.

National Portrait Gallery

Mezzanine level

★ For the Road
The Yeats Museum houses works by Jack B Yeats (1871–1957). This mysterious painting reflects the artist's obsession with the Sligo countryside.

Shaw Room

Merrion Square entrance

STAR PAINTINGS

- ★ The Taking of Christ by Caravaggio

- ★ Pierrot by Juan Gris

- ★ For the Road by Jack Yeats

★ **The Taking of Christ**
Rediscovered in the Dublin Jesuit House of Study in 1990, this 1602 composition by Caravaggio has enhanced the gallery's reputation.

The Millennium Wing, a new airy entrance court, has provided the gallery with space to showcase major travelling shows.

Level 2

Judith with the Head of Holofernes
This monochrome image by Andrea Mantegna (c. 1431–1506) depicts the decapitation of an Assyrian chief.

Level 1

The Sick Call
Painted in a Pre-Raphaelite style by Matthew James Lawless, this 1863 canvas evokes the suffering of the Irish population in the years following the Famine.

Entrance level

Main entrance (Clare Street)

KEY TO FLOORPLAN

▢ Irish School	▢ Spanish School
▢ British School	▢ Northern European Schools
▢ Portraiture	▢ Baroque
▢ European Sculpture and Decorative Arts	▢ Yeats Museum
▢ Print Gallery	▢ Temporary exhibitions
▢ Italian School	▢ Non-exhibition space
▢ French School	

Exploring the National Gallery

Exhibitions throughout the gallery are laid out in an easy-to-follow manner. In addition to rooms dedicated to major Irish and European schools, there are displays illustrating such themes as art in the Dutch provinces, Caravaggio and his followers and Italian influences in the Northern countries. Major temporary exhibitions are held in the Millennium Wing, which also has a floor dedicated to the Irish schools of the 20th century.

IRISH SCHOOL

This is the largest collection on display and the richest part of the gallery. Stretching back to the late 17th century, works range from landscapes such as *A View of Powerscourt Waterfall* by George Barret to paintings by Nathaniel Hone the Elder, including *The Conjuror*. Portraiture includes work by James Barry and Hugh Douglas Hamilton.

The Romantic movement made a strong impression on artists in the early 19th century; Francis Danby's *The Opening of the Sixth Seal*, an apocalyptic interpretation from the Book of Revelations, is the best example of this genre. Other examples are the Irish landscapes of James Arthur O'Connor.

In the late 19th century many Irish artists lived in Breton colonies, absorbing Impressionist influences. Roderic O'Conor's *Farm at Lezaven, Finistère* and William Leech's *Convent Garden, Brittany*, with its

Convent Garden, Brittany, by William Leech (1881–1968)

refreshing tones of green and white, are two of the best examples from this period.

Jack B Yeats is regarded as Ireland's first internationally known modern artist and the Yeats Museum is dedicated to him and his talented family. It includes works by Anne Yeats and his father John B Yeats, a famous portrait artist. Jack B Yeats' paintings portray life in the west of Ireland in the early 20th century. His later paintings, such as *Men of Destiny* and *Above the Fair*, are also national treasures.

BRITISH SCHOOL

Works dating from the 18th century dominate in those rooms that are devoted to British artists. In particular, William Hogarth, Thomas Gainsborough and Joshua Reynolds are well represented. Reynolds was one of the great portrait painters of his time, but the gallery also showcases other portraits, by artists such as Philip Reinagle, Francis Wheatley and Henry Raeburn, that perfectly capture the family, military and aristocratic life of that period.

BAROQUE GALLERY

This large room accommodates 17th-century paintings, many by lesser-known artists. It also holds enormous canvases by more famous names such as Lanfranco, Jordaens and Castiglione, which are too big to fit into the spaces occupied by their respective schools. *The Annunciation* and *Peter Finding the Tribute Money* by Rubens are among the gallery's most eye-catching paintings.

FRENCH SCHOOL

The paintings in the galleries devoted to the French School are separated into the 17th and 18th centuries and the Barbizon, Impressionist, post-Impressionist and Cubist collections.

Among the earlier works are *The Annunciation*, a fine 15th-century panel by Jacques Yverni, and the *Lamentation over the Dead Christ* by Nicolas Poussin (1594–1665), one of the founders of European classicism.

The early 19th century saw the French colonization of North Africa. Many works were inspired by the colonization, including *Guards at the Door of a Tomb*, a painting by Jean-Léon Gérôme. Another fine 19th-century work is the painting known as *A Group of Cavalry in the Snow* by Jan Chelminski.

A View of Powerscourt Waterfall by George Barret the Elder (c.1728–84)

A Group of Cavalry in the Snow by Jan Chelminski (1851–1925)

The Impressionist paintings are among the most popular in the gallery and include Monet's *A River Scene, Autumn* from 1874. Works by Pissarro and Sisley are also displayed in this set of rooms.

Guards at the Door of a Tomb by Jean-Léon Gérôme (1824–1904)

SPANISH SCHOOL

Works from the Spanish school are rich and varied. One of the early pieces of note is El Greco's *St Francis Receiving the Stigmata*, a particularly dramatic work, dating from around 1595. Other notable acquisitions from this period are by Zurbarán, Velázquez and Murillo. There are four works on display by the controversial court painter Francisco de Goya (1746–1828) including a portrait of the actress Doña Antonia Zárata. Pablo Picasso's *Still Life With A Mandolin* and *Pierrot* by Juan Gris represent 20th-century Spanish art.

ITALIAN SCHOOL

As a result of a successful purchasing strategy at the time of the gallery's inauguration and various bequests, there is a strong collection of Italian art in the gallery.

Works of the Italian School spread over seven rooms. Andrea Mantegna's *Judith with the Head of Holofernes* is done in *grisaille*, a technique that creates a stone-like effect. Famous pieces by Uccello, Titian, Moroni and Fontana hang in this section, but it is Caravaggio's *The Taking of Christ* (1602) which is the most important item. It was discovered by chance in a Dublin Jesuit house where it had hung in obscurity for many years. It was first hung in the National Gallery in 1993.

Constantinople School icon

NORTHERN EUROPEAN SCHOOLS

The early Netherlandish School is comprised largely of paintings with a religious theme. One exception is Brueghel the Younger's lively *Peasant Wedding* (1620). In the Dutch collection there are many 17th-century works, including some by Rembrandt. Other highlights include *A Wooded Landscape* by Hobbema and *Lady Writing a Letter With Her Maid* by Vermeer. Rubens and van Dyck are two more famous names here, but there are also fine works by less well-known artists, such as van Uden's *Peasants Merry-making*. Portraits by artists such as Faber and Pencz from the 15th and 16th centuries dominate the German collection, though Emil Nolde's colourful *Two Women in the Garden* dates from 1915.

PORTRAITURE

The impressive Shaw Room is lined with full-length historical portraits including one of Charles Coote, the first Earl of Bellamont, dressed in flamboyant pink ceremonial robes. In the National Portrait Gallery, portraits of those who have made a contribution to Ireland from the 16th century to the present are displayed.

Peasant Wedding by Pieter Brueghel the Younger (1564–1637)

SOUTHWEST DUBLIN

The area around Dublin Castle was first settled in prehistoric times, and it was from here that the city grew. Dublin gets its name from the dark pool *(Dubh Linn)* which formed at the confluence of the Liffey and the Poddle, a river that originally ran through the site of Dublin Castle. It is now channelled underground. Archaeological excavations behind Wood Quay, on the banks of the river Liffey, reveal that the Vikings had a settlement here as early as AD 841.

Following Strongbow's invasion of 1170, a medieval city began to emerge; the Anglo-Normans built strong defensive walls around the castle.

Vibrant artwork typical of shops and galleries in Temple Bar

A small reconstructed section of these old city walls can be seen at St Audoen's Church. More conspicuous reminders of the Anglo-Normans appear in the medieval Christ Church Cathedral and St Patrick's Cathedral. When the city expanded during the Georgian era, the narrow cobbled streets of Temple Bar became a quarter inhabited by skilled craftsmen and merchants. Today this area is considered to be the trendiest part of town, and is home to a variety of alternative shops and cafés. The Powerscourt Townhouse is an elegant 18th-century mansion that has been converted into one of the city's best shopping centres.

SIGHTS AT A GLANCE

Museums and Libraries
Chester Beatty Library ❷
Dublinia ⓭
Marsh's Library ❽

Historic Buildings
City Hall ❸
Dublin Castle pp56–7 ❶
Olympia Theatre ❺
Powerscourt Townhouse ❻
Tailors' Hall ⓫

Historic Areas
Temple Bar pp58–9 ❹

Churches
Christ Church Cathedral pp64–5 ⓮
St Audoen's Church ⓬
St Patrick's Cathedral ❾
St Werburgh's Church ❿
Whitefriar Street Carmelite Church ❼

0 metres 250
0 yards 250

KEY

▮ Street-by-Street map
See pp54–5

GETTING AROUND
Buses 11, 16A, 16B, 19A, 121, 122 and 123 go close to Temple Bar. Buses 49A, 49B, 54A, 65A, 65B, 77 and 123 go past St Patrick's and Christ Church cathedrals.

◁ **Colourful street in bustling Temple Bar**

Street-by-Street: Southwest Dublin

Despite its wealth of ancient buildings, such as Dublin Castle and Christ Church Cathedral, this part of Dublin lacks the sleek appeal of the neighbouring streets around Grafton Street. In recent years, however, redevelopment has rejuvenated the area, especially around Temple Bar, where the attractive cobbled streets are lined with shops, futuristic arts centres, galleries, bars and cafés.

Sunlight Chambers
Built in 1900, the delightful terra-cotta decoration on the façade advertises Lever's soap manufacturing business.

Wood Quay is where the Vikings established their first permanent settlement in Ireland around 841.

Dublin Viking Adventure

★ Christ Church Cathedral
Huge family monuments, including that of the 19th Earl of Kildare, can be found in Ireland's oldest cathedral, which also has a fascinating crypt **14**

St Werburgh's Church
An ornate interior hides behind the somewhat drab exterior of this 18th-century church **10**

Dublinia
Medieval Dublin is the subject of this interactive museum, located in the former Synod Hall of the Church of Ireland. It is linked to Christ Church by a bridge **13**

City Hall
Originally built as the Royal Exchange in 1779, the city's municipal headquarters is fronted by a huge Corinthian portico **3**

★ Dublin Castle
The Drawing Room, with its Waterford crystal chandelier, is part of a suite of luxurious rooms built in the 18th century for the Viceroys of Ireland **1**

O'Connell Bridge

Ha'penny Bridge

Millennium Bridge

QUAY

TEMPLE BAR

CROWN ALLEY

FOWNES ST

SYCAMORE ST

EUSTACE STREET

TEMPLE LANE

DAME STREET

STH GT GEORGE'S ST

DAME CT

EXCHEQUER ST

DRURY ST

WILLIAM ST SOUTH

LOCATOR MAP
See Street Finder map pp180–81

NORTH OF THE LIFFEY

SOUTHWEST DUBLIN

SOUTHEAST DUBLIN

★ Temple Bar
This arts and entertainment district occupies a maze of narrow cobbled streets ❹

Central Bank of Ireland

Irish Film Centre

The Covered Market
This market is a popular spot for buying second-hand clothes and antique jewellery.

Powerscourt Townhouse
This shopping centre is one of the best places in Dublin to find fashion accessories and arts and crafts ❻

→ Grafton Street

0 metres   50
0 yards   50

Olympia Theatre
This Victorian venue stages live comedy, dramatic performances and concerts ❺

The Long Hall
This is a magnificent, old-fashioned pub. Behind the narrow room's long bar stands a bewildering array of antique clocks.

The Long Hall

KEY

– – – Suggested route

STAR SIGHTS

★ Dublin Castle

★ Temple Bar

★ Christ Church Cathedral

Dublin Castle ❶

St Patrick by
Edward Smyth

Dublin gets its name from the ancient black pool harbour, or *Dubb Linn*, that occupied the site of the present castle gardens. Part of the town's 10th-century defence bank is visible at the undercroft. The upper castle yard corresponds closely to the castle established by King John in 1204, which became the most important fortification in Ireland and was the seat of colonial rule and the centre of military, political and social affairs. On the castle's southern side, the magnificent state apartments include St Patrick's Hall and the drawing and throne rooms. They were built as the residential quarters of the viceregal court and now host important state functions.

Figure of Justice
Facing the Upper Yard above the main entrance from Cork Hill, this statue aroused much cynicism among Dubliners, who felt she was turning her back on the city.

★ **Throne Room**
Built in 1740, this room contains a throne said to have been presented by William of Orange after his victory at the Battle of the Boyne (see p15).

Ship Street
Gate

Portrait
Gallery

Bedford Tower
(1761)

Entrance
from
Cork Hill

Entrance to
state apartments

Upper yard

Bermingham
Tower
(1777)

Entrance to
upper yard

Undercroft

Octagonal
Tower (c. 1812)

Record Tower (1226)

★ **St Patrick's Hall**
This hall, with its banners of the now defunct Knights of St Patrick, has ceiling paintings by Vincenzo Valdré (1778), symbolizing the relationship between Britain and Ireland.

The Chapel Royal was completed in 1814 by Francis Johnston. The 100 heads on the exterior of this Neo-Gothic church were carved by Edward Smyth.

ROBERT EMMET

Robert Emmet (1778–1803),
son of the state physician
to the viceroy, led a failed
attack on Dublin Castle
in 1803. He was arrested
and interrogated in the
Record Tower. His final
defiant and patriotic speech
proved an inspiration to
future generations of Irish
freedom fighters. Publicly
hung, drawn and quartered,
the heroic Emmet became
known as "the father of
Irish Republicanism".

Treasury
building

Lower yard

Dame Street
and Palace
Street Gate

STAR FEATURES

★ St Patrick's Hall

★ Throne Room

Manuscript (1874) from the Holy Koran written by calligrapher Ahmad
Shaikh in Kashmir, Chester Beatty Library

Chester Beatty
Library ❷

Clock Tower Building, Dubh Linn
Gardens, Dublin Castle. **Map** C4.
Tel 407 0750. May–Sep: 10am–
5pm Mon– Fri; Oct–Apr: 10am–5pm
Tue–Fri; 11am–5pm Sat, 1pm–5pm
Sun all year. public hols.
www.cbl.ie

This world-renowned
collection of Oriental manuscripts and art was named
European Museum of the Year
in 2002. It was bequeathed to
Ireland by American mining
magnate Sir Alfred Chester
Beatty, who died in 1968.
This generous act no doubt
led to his selection as Ireland's
first honorary citizen in 1957.
During his lifetime Beatty
accumulated almost 300 copies
of the Koran, representing the
works of master calligraphers
from Iran, Turkey and the
Arab world. Other exhibits
include some 6,000-year-old
Babylonian stone tablets,
Greek papyri dating from the
2nd century AD and biblical
material written in Coptic, the
original language of Egypt.
In the Far Eastern collection
is a display of Chinese jade
books – each leaf is made from
thinly cut jade. Burmese and
Siamese art is represented in
the fine collection of 18th-
and 19th-century Parabaiks,
books of illustrated folk tales.
The Japanese collection also
includes many books as well
as paintings from the 16th to
the 18th centuries.

Turkish and Persian
miniatures, striking Buddhist
paintings and Chinese dragon
robes are among many other
fascinating exhibits in this
unusual museum.

City Hall ❸

Cork Hill, Dame St. **Map** C3. **Tel** 222
2204. 10am–5:15pm Mon–Sat,
2–5pm Sun, public hols. Good
Fri, 24th–26th Dec.
www.dublincity.ie/cityhall

Designed by Thomas Cooley,
this imposing building was
built between 1769 and 1779
as the Royal Exchange. It was
taken over by Dublin
Corporation in 1852 as a meeting place for the city council,
a role it keeps to this day.
Tours are available of the
building, recently restored to
its original condition. *Dublin
City Hall – The Story of the
Capital*, is a permanent
exhibition housed in the
lower ground floor covering
1,000 years of history.

Façade of City Hall

Temple Bar ❹

The cobbled streets between Dame Street and the Liffey are named after Sir William Temple who acquired the land in the early 1600s. The term "bar" meant a riverside path. In the 1800s it was home to small businesses but over the years went into decline. In the early 1960s the land was bought up with plans to build a new bus station. Artists and retailers took short-term leases but stayed on when the redevelopment plans were scrapped. Temple Bar prospered and today it is an exciting place, with bars, restaurants, shops and galleries. Stylish and eco-friendly architectural development is contributing further to the area's appeal.

Palm tree seat

Modern, floor-lit entrance hall of the Irish Film Institute

Exploring Temple Bar

The most dramatic way to enter Temple Bar is through the **Merchants' Arch** opposite Ha'penny Bridge *(see p77)*. Underneath the arch is a short, dark alley lined with bazaar-like retail outlets. The alley opens out into the modern airy space of **Temple Bar Square**, a popular lunchtime hangout, where there is a small but eclectic **book market** at weekends. Along the east side is **Crown Alley** with its brightly painted shops and cafés.

Galleries and gallery shops abound. In the northwest corner of the square is the **Temple Bar Gallery and Studios**, a renovated factory that combines exhibition and studio spaces. The **Original Print Gallery** on Temple Bar street and the **Graphic Studio Gallery** off Cope Street sell handmade prints.

The **Contemporary Music Centre**, on Fishamble Street, is Ireland's national archive and resource centre for new music, supporting the work of composers throughout Ireland. The **Temple Bar Information Centre**, on East Essex Street, provides details of arts, culture and entertainment in the area.

Near Christ Church Cathedral in the Old City district, is **Cow's Lane**, a new pedestrian street complete with designer shops and its own fashion and design market every Saturday.

In the evening, there are a huge number of restaurants, bars and pubs to choose from, many with live jazz, rock, and traditional Irish music. The **Temple Bar Music Centre** offers an exciting mix of mainly homegrown talent, playing everything from alternative to R&B and garage. They also have a weekly salsa night. For international names, try the

The Temple Bar logo

Olympia Theatre, where the world's biggest bands have played. This Victorian theatre also stages comedy, musicals and, occasionally, drama.

Meeting House Square

Named after a Quaker place of worship which once stood here, this outdoor performance space is a wonderful asset to the city. It is one of the main venues for Diversions, a free outdoor cultural programme that runs from May to September, featuring lunchtime and evening concerts, and open-air theatre. Screenings of films and numerous family events also take place in the square. Every Saturday, an excellent gourmet food market is held here.

Project

39 East Essex Street. **Tel** 881 9613/14. ☐ *11am–7pm Mon–Sat; shows nightly.* ⚫ ☐ ☐ **www**.project.ie
Begun in 1966, Project has developed from a voluntary, artist-led co-operative to a modern arts centre, with an international reputation for avant garde theatre, dance, music, film and visual art. Project has launched the careers of actors Gabriel Byrne and Liam Neeson, and even U2 cut their teeth here. It also runs a weekly clubnight. Perfomance and exhibition space in the custom-designed building is flexible and fluid, allowing room for artistic invention.

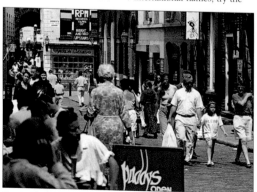

Shoppers in the streets of Temple Bar

Gallery of Photography

Meeting House Square. *Tel 671 4654.*
◯ *11am–6pm Tue–Sat, 1–6pm Sun.*
▢ www.galleryofphotography.ie
This bright, contemporary
space runs exhibitions of high
quality Irish and international
photography, some of which
feature talks by the artist
exhibiting. The shop has an
extensive selection of photos,
postcards and specialist titles.

National Photographic Archive

Meeting House Square. *Tel 603
0374.* ◯ *10am–5pm Mon–Fri,
10am–2pm Sat.* www.nli.ie
The National Library's
collection of around 300,000
photographs is housed here.
The Archive has rolling
exhibitions, mainly featuring
items from the collections.
Subject matter ranges from
social and political history to
early tourist postcards and
dramatic landscape shots,
offering a window into a time
when Ireland really was a
land of thatched cottages
and donkey carts.

Irish Film Institute

6 Eustace Street. *Tel 679 5744.*
◯ *daily.* ▢ ▢ www.irishfilm.ie
Opened in November 1992,
in the wake of international
hits such as *The Commitments*
(1991), this was the first major

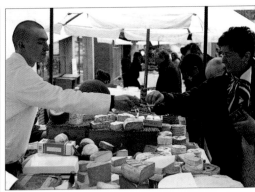

Cheese stall at the weekly gourmet market in Meeting House Square

cultural project completed in
Temple Bar. A neon sign indicates the main entrance, which
runs through a floor-lit corridor
before opening into an airy
atrium where visitors can
browse in the bookshop or
have a snack, meal or drink in
the bar and restaurant. The
IFI's two screens focus on
cult, arthouse and independent
films as well as showing
archive screenings and docu-
mentaries. There are also
seminars, workshops, seasons
on various themes, nations or
directors, and the Jameson
International Film Festival
each year. A small temporary
membership fee is payable
on top of the ticket price.

Cultivate Sustainable Living Centre

15–19 Essex Street West. *Tel 674 5773.*
◯ 11am–6:30pm Mon–Sat (7:30pm
Thurs). ● public hols. ▢
www.sustainable.ie
Learn about the green development of Temple Bar at this
ecological centre with exhibitions, screenings of cutting-
edge films and a demonstration
garden. Interactive maps
show sites of environmental
interest, from bicycle routes
to eco-cultural tourist sites.
Four times a year, Cultivate
hosts the four-day Conver-
gence Festival, highlighting
key ecological issues through
drama, film, live music, art,
workshops and presentations.

TEMPLE BAR

Contemporary Music
  Centre ⑫
Cultivate ⑪
Gallery of Photography ⑧
Graphic Studio Gallery ③
Irish Film Institute ⑨
National Photographic
  Archive ⑤
Olympia Theatre ⑩

Original Print Gallery ①
Project ⑦
Temple Bar Gallery ②
Temple Bar Information
  Centre ⑥
Temple Bar Music
  Centre ④

0 metres   400
0 yards   400

The light and airy interior of Powerscourt Townhouse shopping centre

Olympia Theatre ❺

73 Dame St. **Map** C3. **Tel** 679 3323.
☐ 10:30am–6:30pm Mon–Sat (box
office). See also **Theatre in Dublin**
pp158–9.

Dublin's oldest theatre is a
former Victorian music hall.
The large auditorium is now
used as both a theatre and a
venue for live bands.
    The theatre was
originally built in
1879 by Dan
Lowrey as the Star
of Erin Music Hall
and was eventually
demolished and
rebuilt as the
Olympia Theatre in
1897. Its 19th-
century Victorian
canopy was accidentally
destroyed in 2004 but there
are plans to rebuild it.

**Façade of
Olympia Theatre**

Powerscourt Townhouse ❻

South William St. **Map** D4. **Tel** 671
7000. ☐ 10am–6pm Mon–Fri (8pm
Thu), 9am–6pm Sat, noon–6pm Sun.
See also **Shopping in Dublin** pp148–
51. **www**.powerscourtcentre.com

Completed in 1774 by Robert
Mack, this grand mansion
was originally built as the
city home of Viscount
Powerscourt, who also had a
country estate at Enniskerry,
just south of Dublin. Granite
from the Powerscourt estate
was used in the construction
of this mansion.
    Today the building houses
one of Dublin's best shopping
centres. Inside it still features
the original grand mahogany
    staircase, and finely
    detailed plasterwork
    by stuccodore
    Michael Stapleton.
    In 1807, Powers-
    court Townhouse
    was sold to the
    government, and
    the architect Francis
    Johnston was
    appointed to add
    three groups of
buildings around the courtyard for use as a stamp office,
and to erect the clock tower
and bell on Clarendon Street.
    The building became a dra-
pery warehouse in the 1830s,
and major restoration in the
late 1970s turned it into a
centre of galleries, antique
shops, jewellery stalls and
other shop units. The central
courtyard café, topped by
a glass dome, is a popular
meeting place with many
Dubliners. Another entrance
is via the Johnson Court alley,
just off Grafton Street.

Whitefriar Street Carmelite Church ❼

56 Aungier St. **Map** C4. **Tel** 475
8821. ☐ 8am–6:30pm Mon &
Wed–Fri, 8am–9pm Tue, 8am–7pm
Sat, 8am–7:30pm Sun, 9.30am–1pm
public hols. **www**.carmelites.ie

Designed by George
Papworth, this Catholic
church was built in 1827. It
stands alongside the site of a
medieval Carmelite foundation.
    In contrast to the two
Church of Ireland cathedrals,
St Patrick's and Christ Church,
which are usually full of
tourists, this church is frequented by worshippers from all
over Dublin. Every day they
come to light candles to
various saints, including St
Valentine – the patron saint of
lovers. His remains, previously
buried in the cemetery of St
Hippolytus in Rome, were
offered to the church as a gift
from Pope Gregory XVI in
1836. Today they rest beneath
the commemorative statue to
the saint, which stands in the
northeast corner of the
church beside the high altar.
    Nearby is the figure of Our
Lady of Dublin, a Flemish oak
statue dating from the late 15th
or early 16th century. It may
have belonged to St Mary's
Abbey (see p76) and is thought
to be the only wooden statue
of its kind to have escaped
destruction when Ireland's
monasteries were sacked
during the time of the
Reformation (see p14).

Statue of Our Lady of Dublin in
Whitefriar Street Carmelite Church

The entrance to Marsh's Library, adjacent to St Patrick's Cathedral

Marsh's Library ❽

St Patrick's Close. **Map** B4.
Tel *454 3511.* ◻ *10am–1pm,
2–5pm Mon, Wed–Fri, 10:30am–
1pm Sat.* ● *24 Dec–2 Jan, public
hols.* 🎫 *www.marshlibrary.ie*

Built in 1701 for Archbishop
Narcissus Marsh, this is the
oldest public library in
Ireland. It was designed by
Sir William Robinson, architect of the Royal Hospital
Kilmainham *(see p84).*
    To the rear of the library are
wired alcoves where readers
were locked in with rare
books. The collection of books
from the 16th–18th centuries
includes a volume of
Clarendon's *History of the
Rebellion,* with margin
notes by Jonathan Swift.

St Patrick's Cathedral ❾

St Patrick's Close. **Map** B4. ***Tel*** *475
4817.* ◻ *Mar–Oct: 9am–6pm
Mon–Sat; 9–11am, 12:45–3pm &
4:15–6pm Sun. Nov–Feb: 9am–6pm
Mon–Fri; 9am–5pm Sat; 10–11am &
12:45–3pm Sun. Tours are not
admitted during services.* 🎫 ♿
www.stpatrickscathedral.ie

Ireland's largest church was
founded beside a sacred
well where St Patrick is said
to have baptized converts
around AD 450. The original
building was just a wooden
chapel and remained so until
1192, when Archbishop John
Comyn rebuilt it in stone.
    In the mid-17th century,
Huguenot refugees from
France arrived in Dublin, and

were given the Lady Chapel
by the Dean and Chapter as
their place of worship. The
chapel was separated from the
rest of the cathedral and used
by the Huguenots until the late
18th century. Today St Patrick's
is the Protestant Church of
Ireland's national cathedral.
    Much of the present building
dates back to work completed
between 1254 and 1270. The
cathedral suffered over the
centuries from desecration,
fire and neglect but, thanks to
Sir Benjamin Guinness, it
underwent extensive restoration in the 1860s. The building
is 91 m (300 ft) long; at the
western end is a 43-m (141-ft)
tower, restored by Archbishop
Minot in 1370 and now known
as Minot's Tower. The spire
was added in the 18th century.

The interior is dotted with
memorial busts, brasses and
monuments. A leaflet available at the front desk helps
identify and locate them.
Famous citizens remembered
in the church include the
harpist Turlough O'Carolan
(1670–1738), Douglas Hyde
(1860–1949), the first
President of Ireland and
of course Jonathan Swift
and his beloved Stella.
    At the west end of the nave
is an old door with a hole in
it – a relic from a feud between the Lords Kildare and
Ormonde in 1492. The latter
took refuge in the Chapter
House, but a truce was soon
made and a hole was cut in
the door by Lord Kildare so
that the two could shake
hands in friendship.

JONATHAN SWIFT (1667–1745)

Jonathan Swift was born in Dublin and educated at Trinity
College *(see pp38–9).* He left for England in 1689, but returned in 1694 when his political career failed. He began
a life in the church, becoming Dean of
St Patrick's in 1713. In addition, he
was a prolific political commentator
– his best-known work, *Gulliver's
Travels,* contains a bitter satire on
Anglo-Irish relations. Swift's
personal life, particularly his
friendship with two younger
women, Ester Johnson, better
known as Stella, and Hester
Vanhomrigh, attracted criticism. In
later life, he suffered from Menière's
disease (an illness of the ear), which
led many to believe he was insane.

St Patrick's Cathedral with Minot's Tower and spire

Nave of St Werburgh's Church, showing gallery and organ case

St Werburgh's Church ❿

Entrance through 7–8 Castle St. **Map** C4. **Tel** 478 3710. ◯ 10am–4pm Mon–Fri, ring bell if doors locked.

Built on late 12th-century foundations, St Werburgh's was designed by Thomas Burgh in 1715, after an act of parliament which appointed commissioners to build a new church. Around 85 people made donations. By 1719 the church was complete but had an unfinished tower. Then in 1728 James Southwell bequeathed money for a clock and bells for the church on condition that the tower was completed within three years of his death. It was finally finished in 1732. After a fire in 1754 it was rebuilt with the financial help of George II. It served as the parish church of Dublin Castle, hosting many state ceremonies, including the swearing-in of viceroys. However, this role was later taken over by the Church of the Most Holy Trinity within the castle walls.

Beyond the shabby pallor of its exterior walls lies some fine decorative work. There are massive memorials to members of the Guinness family, and a finely carved Gothic pulpit by Richard Stewart. Also worth seeing are the 1767 organ case and the beautiful stuccowork in the chancel.

Beneath the church lie 27 vaults including that of Lord Edward Fitzgerald, who

died during the 1798 Rebellion (see p16), and also Sir James Ware. The body of Fitzgerald's captor, Major Henry Sirr, is in the graveyard. John Field, the creator of the nocturne, was baptized here in 1782.

Tailors' Hall ⓫

Back Lane. **Map** B4. **Tel** 454 1786. ◯ to the public. **www**.antaisce.org

Dublin's only surviving guild-hall preserves a delightful corner of old Dublin in an otherwise busy redevelopment zone. Built in 1706, it stands behind a limestone arch in a quiet cobbled yard. The building is the oldest guildhall in Ireland and was used by various trade groups including hosiers, saddlers and barber-surgeons as well as tailors. It was regarded as the most fashionable venue in Dublin for social occasions such as balls and concerts for many years until the New Music Hall in Fishamble Street opened and the social scene transferred to there. It also hosted many political meetings – the Protestant leader of the United Irishmen, Wolfe Tone, famously made a speech at the convention of the Catholic Committee on 2nd December 1792 before the 1798 rebellion (see p16).

The building closed in the early 1960s due to neglect, but an appeal by Desmond Guinness saw the hall totally refurbished. Since 1985 is has been the home of An Taisce (the Irish National Trust).

Façade of Tailors' Hall, today the home of the Irish National Trust

St Audoen's Church ⓬

High St, Cornmarket. **Map** B3. **Tel** 677 0088 ◯ Jun–Sep: 9:30am–5:30pm, last adm 4:45pm. ◻ ◻ **www**.heritageireland.ie

Sited in the heart of the walled Medieval City, and designated a National Monument, St Audoen's Church is Dublin's earliest surviving medieval church. It is dedicated to Saint Ouen, the 7th century Bishop of

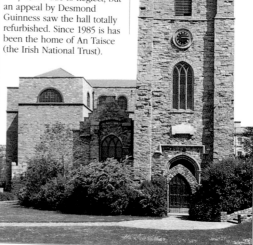

The 12th-century tower of St Audoen's Church, the oldest in Ireland

Rouen and Patron Saint of Normandy. The 15th-century nave remains intact and the three bells date from 1423. The Guild Chapel of St Anne houses an exhibition on the importance of this church in the life of the medieval city. To the rear, steps lead down to St Audoen's Arch, the last remaining gateway of the old city. Flanking the gate are restored sections of the 13th-century city walls.

Next door stands St Audoen's Roman Catholic Church, which was begun in 1841 and completed in 1847. It was built by Patrick Byrne, of Talbot Street, who studied at the Dublin Society School. The parish priest, Patrick Mooney, completed the plasterwork and also installed the organ. In 1884 the dome of the church collapsed and was replaced with a plaster circle. The portico was added to the building in 1899. The Great Bell, dedicated on All Saints Day in 1848 and known as The Liberator after Daniel O'Connell, rang to announce his release from prison and also tolled on the day of his funeral. The two Pacific clam shells by the front of the church hold holy water.

Dublinia ⑬

St Michael's Hill. **Map** B3. **Tel** *679 4611.* ◻ *Apr–Sep: 10am–5pm daily; Oct–Mar: 11am–4pm Mon–Fri, 10am–4pm Sat, Sun & public hols (last adm: 3:15pm).* ● *17 Mar, 23–26 Dec.* ◪ *minimum charge to enter Christ Church Cathedral via bridge.* ◪ *www.dublinia.ie*

Managed by the non-profit-making Medieval Trust, the Dublinia exhibition covers the formative period of Dublin's history from the arrival of the Anglo-Normans in 1170 to the closure of the monasteries in the 1540s. The exhibition is housed in the Neo-Gothic Synod Hall, which, up until 1983, was home to the ruling body of the Church of Ireland. The building and the bridge linking it to Christ Church Cathedral date from the 1870s.

Former Synod Hall, now home to the Dublinia Exhibition

Before Dublinia was established in 1993, the Synod Hall was briefly used as a nightclub.

The exhibition is entered via the basement where visitors walk through life-sized reconstructions of the Medieval City complete with realistic sounds and smells. These depict major events in Dublin's history, such as the Black Death and the rebellion of Silken Thomas *(see p14).* The ground floor houses a large-scale model of Dublin as it was around 1500, and reconstructions including the inside of a late medieval merchant's kitchen. There is also a display of artifacts from the Wood Quay excavation. This was the site of the first Viking settlement in Ireland. Excavations in the 1970s revealed remains of Norse and Norman villages, and artifacts including pottery, swords,

Medieval key in the Dublinia exhibition

coins and leatherwork. Many of these finds are also on display at the National Museum *(see pp44–5).* However, the city chose not to develop the Wood Quay site, but instead built two large civic offices there. If you go to Wood Quay today all you will find is a plaque and an unusual picnic site by the Liffey in the shape of a Viking longboat.

Also in the exhibition are information panels on the themes of trade, merchants and religion. On the first floor is the wood-panelled Great Hall, one of the finest examples of Victorian Gothic style in Dublin. From Easter 2005 the Great Hall will house *The Viking World,* an exhibition exploring the impact of the Vikings on those they encountered and the legacy they left behind. This exhibition will complement the one on medieval Dublin, providing an overview of the city during the Viking and medieval period.

Mid 13th-century jug in Dublinia

Reconstruction of a Viking street in Dublinia

Christ Church Cathedral ⑭

Christ Church Cathedral was established by the Hiberno-Norse king of Dublin, Sitric "Silkbeard", and the first bishop of Dublin, Dunan. It was rebuilt by the Anglo-Norman archbishop, John Cumin from 1186. It is the cathedral for the Church of Ireland (Anglican) diocese of Dublin and Glendalough. By the 19th century it was in a bad state of repair, but was completely remodelled by architect George Street in the 1870s. The vast 12th-century crypt was restored in 2000.

Arms on Lord Mayor's pew

★ **Medieval Lectern**
This beautiful brass lectern was hand-made during the Middle Ages. It stands on the north side of the nave, in front of the pulpit. The matching lectern on the south side is Victorian.

The Lord Mayor's pew is usually kept in the north aisle, but is moved to the front of the nave when used by Dublin's civic dignitaries. It features a carving of the city arms and a stand for the civic mace.

Nave
The 25-m (68-ft) high nave has some fine early Gothic arches. On the north side, the 13th-century wall leans out by as much as 50 cm (18 in) due to the weight of the original roof.

Entrance

★ **Strongbow Monument**
The large effigy in chain armour is probably not Strongbow (see p14). However, his remains are buried in the cathedral and the curious half-figure may be part of his original tomb.

The bridge to the Synod Hall was added when the cathedral was being rebuilt in the 1870s.

STAR FEATURES

★ Strongbow Monument

★ Crypt

★ Medieval Lectern

Chapel of St Laud
The casket on the wall contains the heart of St Laurence O'Toole. The chapel features original medieval floor tiles.

VISITORS' CHECKLIST

Christchurch Place. **Map** B3.
Tel 677 8099. 50, 66, 77 &
many other routes. 9:45am–
5pm daily (Jun–Aug: 9am–6pm
daily). 26 Dec. 10am
and 12:45pm Mon–Fri, 11am
and 3:30pm Sun. limited.
www.cccdub.ie

The Lady Chapel is used to celebrate the daily Eucharist.

★ Crypt
This decorated plate by Francis Garthorne is part of a collection presented to Christ Church Cathedral by King William III to mark his victory at the Battle of the Boyne in 1690.

Stairs to crypt

Crypt

The foundations of the original chapter house date back to the late 13th century.

Romanesque Doorway
Leading to the south transept, this ornately carved doorway is one of the finest examples of 12th-century Irish stonework.

TIMELINE

	c.1240 Completion of stone cathedral	**1600** Shopkeepers rent crypt space		**1689** King James II of England worships in cathedral	**1983** Cathedral ceases using Synod Hall
c.1030 Construction of original Viking cathedral		**1541** King Henry VIII alters constitution of cathedral			
1000	**1200**	**1400**	**1600**	**1800**	
1186 The first Anglo-Norman archbishop, John Cumin, begins work on the new cathedral	*Meeting takes place between Lambert Simnel and the Earl of Kildare*	**1487** Coronation of 10-year-old Lambert Simnel as "King of England"	**1742** Choir participates in first performance of Handel's Messiah		**1871** Major rebuilding of the cathedral begins, including Synod Hall and bridge

NORTH OF THE LIFFEY

Dublin's north side was the last part of the city to be developed during the 18th century. The city authorities envisioned an elegant area of leafy avenues, but the reality of today's traffic has rather spoiled their original plans. Nonetheless, O'Connell Street is an impressive thoroughfare, lined with department stores, monuments and historic public buildings.

There are many notable buildings in the area, such as James Gandon's

Bookshop sign on Ormond Quay Lower

glorious Custom House and majestic Four Courts, together with the famous General Post Office, or GPO *(see p71)*. The Rotunda Hospital, Europe's first purpose-built maternity hospital, is another fine building. Dublin's two most celebrated theatres, the Abbey and the Gate, act as cultural magnets, as do the Dublin Writers' Museum and the James Joyce Cultural Centre, two museums that are dedicated to writers who spent most of their lives in the city.

SIGHTS AT A GLANCE

Historic Buildings
Chief O'Neill's
  Viewing Tower **9**
Custom House **1**
Four Courts **12**
King's Inns **8**
Tyrone House **4**

Historic Streets and Bridges
Ha'penny Bridge **16**
O'Connell Street **3**
Parnell Square **7**
Smithfield **10**

Theatres
Abbey Theatre **2**

Churches
St Mary's Church **15**
St Mary's Pro-Cathedral **5**
St Michan's Church **13**

Museums and Galleries
Old Jameson Distillery **11**
James Joyce Cultural Centre **6**
St Mary's Abbey Exhibition **14**

GETTING AROUND
Numerous buses, including the 3, 10, 11, 13, 16 and 16A, go along O'Connell Street and round Parnell Square. To get to Smithfield, take a 67A, 68, 69, 79 or 90. The Tallaght to Connolly Station Luas line runs through the area.

KEY

| | Street-by-Street map See pp68–9 |
| Coach station |
| Luas stop |
| Tourist information |

0 metres 250
0 yards 250

◁ **Portico of the Custom House, illuminated at night**

Street-by-Street: Around O'Connell Street

Throughout the Georgian era, O'Connell Street was the fashionable part of Dublin in which to live. However, the 1916 Easter Rising destroyed many of its fine buildings, including much of the General Post Office – only its original façade remains. Today, this main thoroughfare is lined with shops and businesses. Other nearby attractions include St Mary's Pro-Cathedral and James Gandon's Custom House, overlooking the Liffey.

Pavement mosaic, Moore Street

James Joyce Cultural Centre
This well-restored Georgian town house contains a small Joyce museum ❻

Parnell Monument (1911)

The Gate Theatre was founded in 1928 and is renowned for its productions of contemporary drama.

The Rotunda Hospital
Housing a chapel built in the 1750s to the design of German architect Richard Castle, this hospital features lovely stained-glass windows, fluted columns, panelling and intricate iron balustrades.

Moore Street Market
Be prepared for the cries of the stall holders offering an enormous variety of fresh fruit, vegetables and cut flowers.

The Monument of Light, an elegant stainless steel spire, rises to 120 m (394 ft).

The General Post Office, the grandest building on O'Connell Street, was the centre of the 1916 Rising.

James Larkin Statue (1981)

KEY

— Suggested route

🚋 Luas stop

ℹ Tourist information

0 metres   50

0 yards   50

STAR SIGHTS

★ Custom House

★ O'Connell Street

St Mary's Pro-Cathedral
*Built around 1825, this is
Dublin's main place of
worship for Catholics. The
plaster relief above the
altar in the sanctuary
depicts* The Ascension ❺

LOCATOR MAP
See Street Finder map pp180–81

The statue of James Joyce (1990)
*This work by Marjorie Fitzgibbon
commemorates one of Ireland's most
famous novelists. Born in Dublin in
1882, Joyce catalogued the people and
streets of Dublin in his celebrated books.*

Abbey Theatre
*Ireland's national
theatre is known
throughout the world
for its productions by
Irish playwrights,
such as Sean O'Casey
and JM Synge* ❷

★ O'Connell Street
*This monument to Daniel
O'Connell by John Foley took
19 years to complete from the
laying of its foundation
stone in 1864* ❸

CUSTOM HOUSE QUAY

Butt Bridge

★ Custom House
*This striking head, by
Edward Smyth, symbolizes
the River Liffey. It is one of
14 carved keystones that
adorn the building* ❶

O'Connell
Bridge

Trinity
College

Illuminated façade of the Custom House reflected in the Liffey

Custom House ❶

Custom House Quay. **Map** E2.
Tel 888 2538. ☐ 10am–12:30pm
*Mon–Fri (Nov–Mar: Wed–Fri),
2–5pm Sat, Sun.* 🚫 ♿ weekdays.

This majestic building was
designed as the Custom
House by the English architect
James Gandon. However, the
1800 Act of Union (*see p16*)
transferred the custom and
excise business to London,
rendering the building practic-
ally obsolete. In 1921, Sinn
Féin voters celebrated their
election victory by setting light
to what they saw as a symbol
of British imperialism. The fire
blazed for five days causing
extensive damage. Reconstruction took place in 1926, but the
building was not completely
restored until 1991, when it reopened as government offices.
    The main façade is made
up of pavilions at each end
with a Doric portico in its
centre. The arms of Ireland
crown the two pavilions, and
a series of 14 allegorical
heads by Dublin sculptor
Edward Smyth form the keystones of arches and
entrances. These

heads depict Ireland's main
rivers and the Atlantic Ocean.
A statue of Commerce tops
the central copper dome.
    The best view of the building
is from the south of the Liffey
beyond Matt Talbot Bridge.

Logo of the Abbey Theatre

Abbey Theatre ❷

26 Lower Abbey St. **Map** E2. *Tel* 878
7222 Box office. ☐ *for performances,
some tours. See also* Entertainment
pp154–9. **www**.abbeytheatre.ie

Founded in 1898 with WB
Yeats and Lady Gregory as
co-directors, the Abbey staged

its first play in 1904.
The early years of this
much lauded national
theatre saw works by
W B Yeats, J M Synge
and Sean O'Casey.
Many were contro-
versial: nationalist
sensitivities were
severely tested in 1926
at the premiere of
O'Casey's *The Plough
and the Stars*, when
the flag of the Irish
Free State appeared in
a scene featuring a
pub frequented by prostitutes.
    While presenting the
work of eminent foreign
authors from time to time,
the prime objective of the
Abbey, and the smaller
Peacock Theatre downstairs,
is to provide a performance
space for Irish dramatic
writing. Some of the most
acclaimed performances
have been Brian Friel's
Dancing At Lughnasa,
Patrick Kavanagh's *Tarry
Flynn, The Colleen Bawn* by
Dion Boucicault and Hugh
Leonard's *Love in the Title*.

O'Connell Street ❸

Map D1–D2.

O'Connell Street is very
different from the original
plans of Irish aristocrat Luke
Gardiner. When he bought
the land in the 18th century,
Gardiner envisioned a grand
residential parade with an
elegant mall running
along its centre.
Such plans were
short-lived.
The

O'Connell Bridge spanning the Liffey, viewed from the Butt Bridge construction of Carlisle (now O'Connell) Bridge in 1790 transformed the street into the city's main north-south route. Also, several buildings were destroyed during the 1916 Easter Rising and the Irish Civil War. Since the 1960s many of the old buildings have been replaced by the plate glass and neon of fast food joints and amusement arcades.

A few venerable buildings remain, such as the General Post Office (1818), Gresham Hotel (1817), Clery's department store (1822) and the Royal Dublin Hotel, part of which occupies the street's only original townhouse.

A walk down the central mall is the most enjoyable way to see the street's mix of architectural styles. At the south end stands a huge monument to Daniel O'Connell *(see p16)*, unveiled in 1882. The street, which throughout the 19th century had been called Sackville Street, was renamed for O'Connell in 1922. Higher up, almost facing the General Post Office, is an expressive statue of James Larkin (1867–1943),

Clock outside Clery's department store

leader of the Dublin general strike in 1913. The next statue is of Father Theobald Mathew (1790–1856), founder of the Pioneer Total Abstinence Movement. At the north end of the street is the obelisk-shaped monument to Charles Stewart Parnell (1846–91), who was leader of the Home Rule Party and known as the "uncrowned King of Ireland" *(see p17)*. A new addition to O'Connell Street is the Monument of Light, erected on the site where Nelson's column used to be. The monument is a stainless steel, conical spire which tapers from a three-metre diameter base to a 10-centimetre pointed tip of optical glass at a height of 120 metres.

Tyrone House ❹

Marlborough St. **Map** D2.
🚫 *to the public.*

Considered to be the most important Dublin building by German-born Richard Castle (also known as Cassels) after

Leinster House, this Palladian-style structure was completed around 1740 as a townhouse for Sir Marcus Beresford, later Earl of Tyrone. Its interior features elaborate plasterwork by the Swiss Francini brothers, as well as a grand mahogany staircase. The premises were bought by the government in the 1830s and today house a section of the Department of Education; the minister has one of the most ornate state offices in what used to be a reception room.

Austere Neo-Classical interior of St Mary's Pro-Cathedral

St Mary's Pro-Cathedral ❺

Marlborough St. **Map** D2. **Tel** 874 5441. ⏰ 7:30am–6:45pm Mon–Fri (7:15pm Sat), 9am–1:45pm & 5:30–7:45pm Sun. **www**.procathedral.ie

Dedicated in 1825 before Catholic emancipation *(see p16)*, St Mary's backstreet site was the best the city's Anglo-Irish leaders would allow a Catholic cathedral.

The façade is based on the Temple of Theseus in Athens. Its six Doric columns support a pediment with statues of St Laurence O'Toole, 12th-century Archbishop of Dublin and patron saint of the city, St Mary and St Patrick. The most striking feature of the interior is the intricately carved high altar.

St Mary's is home to the famous Palestrina Choir. In 1904 the great Irish tenor, John McCormack, began his career with the choir, which sings at the 11am Sunday service.

THE GENERAL POST OFFICE (GPO)

Built in 1818 halfway along O'Connell Street, the GPO became a symbol of the 1916 Irish Rising. Members of the Irish Volunteers and Irish Citizen Army seized the building on Easter Monday, and Patrick Pearse *(see p17)* read out the Proclamation of the Irish Republic from its steps. Shelling from the British finally forced the rebels out after a week. At first, many Irish people viewed the Rising unfavourably. However, as WB Yeats wrote, matters "changed utterly" and a "terrible beauty was born" when, during the following weeks, 14 of the leaders were shot at Kilmainham Gaol *(see p81)*. Inside the GPO is a sculpture of the Irish mythical warrior Cúchulainn, dedicated to those who died.

***Irish Life* magazine cover showing the 1916 Easter Rising**

James Joyce Cultural Centre ❻

35 North Great George's St. **Map** D1. *Tel* 878 8547. ⏰ 9:30am–5pm Mon–Sat, 12:30–5pm Sun. ⬤ Good Fri, 23–27 Dec. 📷 ♿ **www**.jamesjoyce.ie

Although born in Dublin, Joyce spent most of his adult life in Europe. He used Dublin as the setting for his major works, including *Ulysses, A Portrait of the Artist as a Young Man* and *Dubliners*.

This centre is located in a 1784 townhouse which was built for the Earl of Kenmare. Michael Stapleton, one of the greatest stuccodores of his time, contributed to the plasterwork with noteworthy friezes.

The main literary display is an absorbing set of biographies of around 50 characters from *Ulysses*, who were based on real Dublin people. Professor Dennis J Maginni, a peripheral character in *Ulysses*, ran a dancing school from this townhouse. Leopold and Molly Bloom, the central characters of *Ulysses*, lived a short walk away at No. 7 Eccles Street. The centre also organizes walking tours of Joyce's Dublin, so a visit is a must for all Joycean zealots.

At the top of the road, on Great Denmark Street, is the Jesuit-run Belvedere College attended by Joyce between 1893 and 1898. He recalls his unhappy schooldays there in *A Portrait of the Artist as a Young Man*. The college's interior contains some of Stapleton's best and most colourful plasterwork (1785).

Portrait of James Joyce (1882–1941) by Jacques Emile Blanche

Parnell Square ❼

Once as affluent as the now-restored squares to the south of the Liffey, Parnell Square is today sadly neglected. However, it still holds many points of interest, including the historic Gate Theatre and the peaceful Garden of Remembrance. There are hopes that this once-elegant part of the city will one day be renovated and restored to its original splendour.

Stained-glass window (c. 1863) in the Rotunda Hospital's chapel

Gate Theatre

1 Cavendish Row. **Map** D1. ⏰ for *performances only.* **Box Office** *Tel* 874 4045. ⏰ 10am–7pm Mon–Sat. See also **Entertainment in Dublin** *pp140–45*. **www**.gate-theatre.ie

Originally the grand supper room in the Rotunda, today the Gate Theatre is renowned for its staging of contemporary international drama in Dublin. It was founded in 1928 by Hilton Edwards and Mícheál Mac Liammóir. The latter is now best remembered for *The Importance of Being Oscar*, his long-running one-man show about the writer Oscar Wilde *(see p23)*. An early success was Denis Johnston's *The Old Lady Says No*, so-called because of the margin notes made on one of his scripts by Lady Gregory, founding director of the Abbey Theatre *(see p70)*. Although still noted for staging productions of new plays, the Gate's current output often includes classic Irish plays including Sean O'Casey's *Juno and the Paycock*.

Entrance to the Gate Theatre

Many famous names in the acting world got their first break at the Gate Theatre, including James Mason and a teenage Orson Welles.

Rotunda Hospital

Parnell Square West. **Map** D1. *Tel* 873 0700.

Standing in the middle of Parnell Square is Europe's first purpose-built maternity hospital. Founded in 1745 by Dr Bartholomew Mosse, the design of the hospital is similar to that of Leinster House *(see p46)*. The German-born architect Richard Castle designed both buildings. At the east end of the hospital is the Rotunda, after which the hospital is named. It was built in 1764 by John Ensor as Assembly Rooms to host fundraising functions and concerts. Franz Liszt gave a concert here in 1843.

On the first floor is a chapel featuring striking stained-glass windows and Rococo plasterwork and ceiling (1755) by the stuccodore Bartholomew

Cramillion. On the other side of the road from the hospital is Conway's Pub. Opened in 1745, it has been popular with expectant fathers for years.

Garden of Remembrance

Parnell Square. **Map** C1.
⬭ *dawn–dusk daily.*
At the northern end of Parnell Square is a small, peaceful park, dedicated to the men and women who have died in the pursuit of Irish freedom. The Garden of Remembrance marks the spot where several leaders of the Easter Rising were held overnight before being taken to Kilmainham Gaol *(see p81)*, and is also where the Irish Volunteers movement was formed in 1913.

Designed by Daithí Hanly, the garden was opened by President Eamon de Valera *(see p18)* in 1966, to mark the 50th anniversary of the Easter Rising. In the centre is a cruciform pool with a mosaic depicting broken swords, shields and spears, symbolizing peace. At one end of the garden is a large bronze sculpture by Oisín Kelly (1971) of the legendary *Children of Lir*, the children of King Lir who were changed into swans by their jealous stepmother.

Gallery of Writers at Dublin Writers' Museum

Dublin Writers' Museum

18 Parnell Square North. **Map** C1.
Tel *872 2077.* ⬭ *Sep–May: 10am–5pm Mon–Sat, 11am–5pm Sun & public hols; Jun–Aug: 10am–6pm Mon–Fri.* ● *25–26 Dec.* 🖾 www.writersmuseum.com
Opened in 1991, the museum occupies an 18th-century townhouse. There are displays relating to Irish literature over the last thousand years, although there is little about writers in the latter part of the 20th century. The exhibits include paintings, manuscripts, letters, rare editions and mementoes of Ireland's finest authors. There are many temporary exhibits and a lavishly decorated Gallery of Writers. The museum also hosts poetry readings and lectures.

Children of Lir in the Garden of Remembrance

There is also a pleasant café and a specialist bookstore, which provides a useful out-of-print search service.

Hugh Lane Municipal Gallery of Modern Art

Charlemont House, Parnell Square North. **Map** C1. **Tel** *222 5550.* ⬭ *10am–6pm Tue–Thu, 10am–5pm Fri, Sat, 11am–5pm Sun.* ● *24–25 Dec, public hols.* 🖾 www.hughlane.ie
Noted art collector Sir Hugh Lane donated his valuable collection of Impressionist paintings to Dublin Corporation in 1905. However, the failure to find a suitable location for them prompted Lane to consider transferring his gift to the National Gallery in London. The Corporation then proposed Charlemont House, the townhouse of Lord Charlemont, who built Marino Casino *(see p88)* and Lane relented. However, in 1915, before Lane's revised will could be witnessed, he died on board the torpedoed liner *Lusitania*. This led to a 50-year dispute which has been resolved by Dublin Corporation and the National Gallery swapping the collection every five years. As well as the Lane bequest the gallery also has a sculpture hall with work by Rodin and others. There is also a collection of modern Irish paintings.

An exciting new addition is the contents of Francis Bacon's studio at 7 Reece Mews, London, donated by Bacon's sole heir, John Edwards, and reconstructed in the Gallery in its entirety.

An extension to the Gallery in May 2006 has doubled the exhibition space.

Sur la Plage (c. 1876) by Edgar Degas, Hugh Lane Municipal Gallery

The impressive façade of the King's Inns, on Constitution Hill

King's Inns ❽

Henrietta St/Constitution Hill.
Map B1. ◐ *to the public, except the gardens.*

This classically proportioned public building was founded in 1795 as a place of both residence and study for barristers in Dublin. The King's Inns was the name taken by the Irish lawyers' society upon Henry VIII declaring himself King of Ireland.

To build it, James Gandon, famous as the architect of the Custom House *(see p70)*, chose to seal off the end of Henrietta Street, which was Dublin's first Georgian street and, at the time, one of the city's most fashionable addresses. In 1816, Francis Johnston added the graceful cupola, and the building was finally completed the following year.

Inside, there is a fine dining hall, and the Registry of Deeds (formerly the Prerogative Court). The west façade has two doorways flanked by elegant Classical caryatids (statues used in place of pillars) carved by sculptor Edward Smyth. The male figure, holding book and quill, is representative of the law.

Statue at the entrance to King's Inns

Sadly, much of the area around Constitution Hill today is less attractive than it was in Georgian times. However, the King's Inns' gardens, which are open to the public, are still pleasant to stroll around.

Chief O'Neill's Viewing Tower ❾

Map A2. **Tel** 817 3838. ◻ 10am–5:30pm Mon–Sat, 11am–5:30pm Sun. ▣

During the past few years, an ongoing programme of urban regeneration has transformed the look of the Smithfield neighbourhood, one of Dublin's oldest trading and residential areas. As part of this programme, the chimney of the Old Jameson Distillery *(see p75)* has been converted into a viewing tower. Now part of the Park Inn Hotel chain, the 56-m (185-ft) tall chimney comprises a glass-walled lift that takes visitors to a two-tiered glass-enclosed viewing platform. From here, vistors can enjoy unique 360-degree panoramic views over the city, as far as Dublin Bay.

Smithfield ❿

Map A2.

Laid out in the mid-17th century as a marketplace, Smithfield used to be one of Dublin's oldest trading and residential areas, playing host to people coming to the cattle- and horsefairs for which the area was famous. The traditional Horsefair still takes place here on the first Sunday of every month, even though the two-and-a-half-acre area has received a £3.5-million makeover and is subject to extensive property development.

The transformation of Smithfield Plaza, commonly known as Smithfield Square, beside the famous fruit and fish markets, is part of Dublin Council's Historical Area Regeneration Programme, a project set up in 1995 in response to the severe decline suffered by the area between 1940 and 1985. The remit of the programme was to make the inner city attractive again.

Children riding saddle-free through the cobbled streets of Smithfield market

The cobbled pedestrian plaza is atmospherically lit by 12 gas lighting masts, each 26 m (85 ft) high, and provides the city with its first dedicated venue for outdoor civic events.

The transformation of Smithfield also includes some riverside public housing, a hotel, several craft shops and a growing selection of bars and restaurants. The area is now said to be the largest purpose-built urban space in Europe, with an expanding legal and commercial district, too.

Old Jameson Distillery ⑪

Bow St. **Map** A2.
Tel 807 2355. ⬜ daily 9am–6pm *(last tour at 5:30pm).* ⬤ Good Fri, *25–26 Dec.* 🎫 ♿ 🍴 🛍
www.jamesonwhiskey.com

Sampling different whiskeys at the Old Jameson Distillery

Proof of significant investment in the emerging Smithfield area of Dublin's northside is evident in this large exhibition, set in a restored building that formed part of John Jameson's distillery. Whiskey was produced here from 1780 until 1971. While the place is run by Irish Distillers Limited, who are obviously keen to talk up their products (the four main names are Jameson, Paddy, Bushmills and John Power), it is an impressive, entertaining and educational experience. Visits start with a video, *Uisce Beatha* (the Water of Life; *uisce* meaning "water"

and the origin of the word "whiskey"). Further whiskey-related facts are then explained to visitors in the 40-minute tour. This moves around displays set out as a working distillery with different rooms devoted to the various stages of whiskey production, from grain storage right through to bottling. The tour guides are keen to point how the barley drying process differs from that used in the production of Scotch whisky: in Ireland the grain is dried through clean dry air while in Scotland it is smoked over peat. They claim that this results in a smoother Irish tipple compared to its more smoky Scottish counterpart. At the end of the tour, visitors can test this claim in the nicely appointed bar.

Horses tethered at the Sunday Horsefair

IRISH WHISKEY

It is widely claimed that the Irish were the first to produce whiskey. This is quite possibly the case, since the monks spreading Christianity across Europe supposedly learnt the skills of distillation in the East where perfume was made. Some even believe that it was St Patrick who introduced the art. In the late 1800s and early 1900s Irish whiskey was superseded somewhat by the lighter blended Scotch. In addition, sales suffered in the United States as a result of the Prohibition. Today however, Irish whiskeys are enjoying a comeback and provide fierce competition for Scotch whiskies.

Old Bushmills *is a blended whiskey made from just one malt and a single grain. The end result is a pleasant blend of malty sweetness and aromatic dryness.*

Jameson 1780, *at 12 years old, has a classic smooth Jameson character. It is a hearty taste of Dublin's distilling heritage.*

Paddy *is the classic whiskey of Cork, Ireland's second city. It is firm-bodied, with the crisp finish typical of native Cork whiskeys.*

Power and Son's *Gold Label Irish, sometimes known as "Three Swallows", is a well-balanced and malty whiskey. Originally from Dublin, today it is very much a national brand.*

James Gandon's Four Courts overlooking the River Liffey

Four Courts ⑫

Inns Quay. **Map** B3. **Tel** 872 5555.
⬭ 9:30am–12:30pm, 2–4:30pm
Mon–Fri (when courts in session).

Completed in 1796 by James Gandon, this majestic building was virtually gutted 120 years later during the Irish Civil War (see p17) when government forces bombarded anti-Treaty rebels into submission. The adjacent Public Records Office, with documents dating back to the 12th century, was destroyed by fire. In 1932, the main buildings were restored using Gandon's original design. A copper-covered lantern dome rises above the six-columned Corinthian portico, which is crowned with the figures of Moses, Justice, Mercy, Wisdom and Authority. This central section is flanked by two wings holding the four original courts: Common Pleas, Chancery, Exchequer and King's Bench. It is possible to walk in to the central waiting hall under the grand dome. An information panel to the right of the entrance details the building's history and functions.

St Michan's Church ⑬

Church St. **Map** B3. **Tel** 872 4154.
⬭ mid-Mar–Oct: 10am–12:45pm, 2–4:45pm Mon–Fri, 10am–12:45pm Sat; Nov–mid-Mar: 12:30–3:30pm Mon–Fri; 10am–12:45pm Sat. ▨ ▨ ▨ ▨ limited.

Largely rebuilt in 1686 on the site of an 11th-century Hiberno-Viking church, the dull façade of St Michan's hides a more exciting interior. Deep in its vaults lie several bodies that have barely decomposed due to the dry atmosphere created by the church's magnesian limestone walls. Their wooden caskets have cracked open, revealing the preserved bodies, complete with skin and hair. Among those thought to have been mummified in this way are the brothers John and Henry Sheares, leaders of the 1798 rebellion (see p16), who were executed that year.

Other, less gory, attractions include the magnificent woodcarving of fruits and violins and other instruments above the choir. There is also an organ (1724) on which Handel is said to have played.

St Mary's Abbey Exhibition ⑭

Meetinghouse Lane. **Map** C2. **Tel** 872 1490. ⬭ mid-Jun–mid-Sep: 10am–5pm Wed, Sun. ▨ **www**.heritageireland.ie

Founded by Benedictine monks in 1139, but then transferred to the Cistercian order eight years later, this was one of the largest and most important monasteries in medieval Ireland. When it was built, the surrounding land was peaceful countryside; to-day, what is left of this historically important abbey is hidden away in

Detail of woodcarving (c. 1724) at St Michan's Church

the sprawling backstreets that are found on the north side of the river Liffey.

As well as having control over extensive estates, including whole villages, mills and fisheries, the abbey acted as state treasury and meeting place for the Council of Ireland. It was during a council meeting in St Mary's that "Silken Thomas" Fitzgerald *(see p14)* renounced his allegiance to Henry VIII and marched out to raise the short-lived rebellion of 1534. The monastery was dissolved a few years later in 1539 and, during the 17th century, the site served as a quarry. Stone from St Mary's was pillaged and used in the construction of Essex Bridge (which was later replaced by Grattan Bridge in 1874), just to the south of the abbey.

Sadly, all that remains of the abbey today is the vaulted chamber of the old Chapter House. This houses a display on the history of the abbey and a model of how it would have looked 800 years ago.

The old vaulted Chapter House in St Mary's Abbey

St Mary's Church 15

Mary St (at Wolfe Tone St). **Map** C2. **Tel** 872 4088.

In among the produce stalls and family-run stores in the warren of streets to the west of O'Connell Street stands what was once one of the most important society churches in 18th- and 19th-century Dublin. Dating back to 1627, its design is usually credited to Sir William Robinson, the Surveyor General who also built the beautiful Royal Hospital Kilmainham *(see p84)*, and it is reckoned to be the first church in the city with a gallery.

Impressive organ in St Mary's Church

Famous past parishioners here include Arthur Guinness, who got married here in 1793, and Wolfe Tone, the leader of the United Irishmen, who was born within a stone's throw of the church and baptized here in the 1760s. The cross street and the small park to the rear of the church are named in his honour today. The playwright Sean O'Casey was also baptized at St Mary's in 1880. Church services finally ceased in the mid-1980s and, since then St Mary's has been through numerous incarnations. Now owned privately, St Mary's opened as a bar and restaurant, Keatings, in 2003. All the listed features were restored by specialist craftsmen. Look out for the organ and impressive stained-glass windows.

Detail of carving in St Mary's Church

Ha'penny Bridge 16

Map D3.

Linking Temple Bar and Liffey Street on the north bank of the river, this attractive high-arched footbridge is made of cast iron and is used by thousands of people every day to cross Dublin's river. It was built by John Windsor, an ironworker from Shropshire, England. One of Dublin's most popular and most photographed sights, it was originally named the Wellington Bridge, after the Duke of Wellington. Its official name today is in fact the Liffey Bridge, but it is also known simply as the Metal Bridge. Originally opened in 1816, the bridge got its better-known nickname from the halfpenny toll that was first levied on it. The toll was scrapped in 1919 but the nickname stuck and is still used with some fondness by Dubliners and visitors alike. A recent restoration job on the bridge, which included the installation of original period lanterns, has made it even more attractive. This is particularly true at night when it is lit up as people cross over it to go through Merchant's Arch and into the bustling nightlife of the Temple Bar area *(see pp58–9)* with all its pubs, clubs and restaurants.

The Ha'penny Bridge looking from Temple Bar to Liffey Street

FURTHER AFIELD

There are many interesting sights just outside Dublin. In the western suburbs is the Museum of Modern Art, housed in the splendid setting of the Royal Hospital Kilmainham. Phoenix Park, Europe's largest city park, offers the opportunity for a stroll in a leafy setting. Further north are the National Botanic Gardens, home to over 20,000 plant species from around the world. Nearby, Marino Casino is

Michael Collins' gravestone

a fine example of Palladian architecture. The magnificent coastline is easily admired by taking the DART railway. The highlight of the riviera-like southern stretch is around Dalkey village, especially lovely Killiney Bay. One of the many Martello towers built as defences now houses a museum to James Joyce. To the northeast, slightly further from the centre, is Malahide Castle, once home of the Talbot family.

SIGHTS AT A GLANCE

Museums and Galleries
Collins Barracks **6**
Fry Model Railway Museum **14**
Guinness Storehouse **4**
James Joyce Tower **17**
Kilmainham Gaol **3**
Irish Museum of Modern Art/
   Royal Hospital Kilmainham **5**

Shaw's Birthplace **7**
Waterways Visitors' Centre **9**

Parks and Gardens
Dublin Zoo **2**
Glasnevin Cemetery **12**
National Botanic Gardens **11**
Phoenix Park **1**

Historic Buildings
Malahide Castle **13**
Marino Casino **10**

Towns and Villages
Ballsbridge **8**
Dalkey **18**
Dun Laoghaire **16**
Howth **15**
Killiney **19**

CENTRAL DUBLIN

GREATER DUBLIN AND ENVIRONS

0 kilometres   4
0 miles   2

KEY

�	Main sightseeing areas
	Greater Dublin
▬	Motorway
▬	Major road
═	Minor road
—	Railway
✈	Dublin airport
⛴	Ferry port
⛴	Fast ferry port

15 km = 10 miles

◁ **Boat moored in Dun Laoghaire harbour at dusk**

Phoenix Park ●

Park Gate, Conyngham Rd, Dublin 8.
🚌 10, 25, 26, 37, 38, 39. ⏰ 7am–
11pm daily. **Phoenix Park Visitor
Centre** **Tel** 677 0095. ⏰ Nov–mid-
Mar: 10am–5pm Sat–Wed; mid- to
end Mar & Oct: 10am–5:30pm
daily; Apr–Sep: 10am–6pm daily
(last adm: 45 mins before closing).
🍴 ♿ 📷 **President's House** 📷
Oct– mid-Apr: 10:30am– 3:30pm Sat;
mid-Apr–Sep: 10:30am– 4:30pm Sat.
www.heritageireland.ie

**The Phoenix Column topped by a
statue of the mythical bird**

To the west of the city centre,
ringed by an 11-km (7-mile)
wall, is Europe's largest
enclosed city park. Phoenix
Park is over 700 ha (1,700
acres) in size. The name
"Phoenix" is said to be a
corruption of the Gaelic *Fionn
Uisce*, meaning "clear water".
The **Phoenix Column** is crowned
by a statue of the mythical bird.

Phoenix Park originated in
1662, when the Duke of
Ormonde turned the land into
a deer park. Deer still roam in
the park today. In 1745 it was
landscaped and opened to the
public by Lord Chesterfield.

Near Park Gate is the lake-
side **People's Garden** – the
only part of the park which
has been cultivated. A little
further on is the
famous **Dublin Zoo**.

In addition to the
Phoenix Column, the
park has two other
striking monuments.
The **Wellington**

Testimonial, a 63-m (204-ft)
obelisk, was begun in 1817
and completed in 1861. It
allegedly took so long to be
built because of the Duke of
Wellington's fall from public
favour. Its bronze bas-reliefs
were made from captured
French cannons. The 27-m
(90-ft) steel **Papal Cross**
marks the spot where Pope
John Paul II celebrated Mass
in front of more than one
million people in 1979.

Most Saturdays, the visitors'
centre issues tickets to the
public for a free guided tour
of **Áras an Uachtaráin**, the
Irish President's official
residence, which was built
within the park in 1751. It
was home to various British
viceroys before becoming the
residence of the president in
1937. **Deerfield**, also dating
to the 18th century, is the
residence of the US Ambass-
ador and was once the home
of Lord Cavendish, the British
Chief Secretary for Ireland
who was murdered in 1882 by
an Irish nationalist. **Ashtown
Castle**, a restored 17th-century

Jogging in Phoenix Park

PHOENIX PARK

Áras An Uachtaráin ⑤
Ashtown Castle ①
Deerfield ②
Dublin Zoo ⑥
Papal Cross ③
People's Garden ⑧
Phoenix Column ④
Wellington Testimonial ⑦

KEY

🚌 Bus stop

🅿 Parking

ℹ Tourist information

▭▭▭ Park wall

| 0 metres | 500 |
| 0 yards | 500 |

NAVAN (N3)
Ashtown Gate
CASTLEKNOCK ROAD
BLACKHORSE
Castleknock Gate
Whites Gate
CHESTERFIELD
AVENUE
Cabra Gate
AVENUE
Knockmaroon Gate
CHESTERFIELD
AVENUE
KNOCKMAROON HILL
NCR Gate
Islandbridge Gate
Park Gate
CONYNGHAM RD
DUBLIN
West Link (M50)
Chapelizod Gate
CHAPELIZOD   ROAD
Liffey
NAAS (N7)

Orang-utan mother and baby at Dublin Zoo

tower house, is adjacent to the Phoenix Park Visitor Centre.

Five times the size of Hyde Park in London and over double the size of New York's Central Park, Phoenix Park can fit playing fields for Gaelic football, hurling and polo, plus running, cycling and horseriding trails.

Visitors watching giraffe at Dublin Zoo

Dublin Zoo ❷

Phoenix Park, Dublin 8. *Tel* 474 8900. ▦ 10, 10A, 25, 25A, 26, 66, 66A, 66B, 67, 67A, 68, 69, 90. ⭘ Mar–Sep: 9:30am–6pm daily (from 10:30am Sun); Oct–Feb: 9:30am–dusk daily (from 10:30am Sun). ♿🍴🛍 www.dublinzoo.ie

Opened in 1830 with one wild boar and an admission price of 6d (2.5 pence), Dublin Zoo was one of the world's first zoos. In its long history, there have been many changes, and today's facility would be unrecognizable to its first visitors.

A recent development is the impressive African Plains sector. This 13-ha (32-acre) savannah, with a large lake and mature woodland, has doubled the size of the zoo and is home to giraffe, rhino, lion, zebra, hippo and cheetah. Other sectors include the World of Primates, World of Cats, and Fringes of the Arctic, with highlights such as the orang-utan, Sumatran tiger, snow leopard and grey wolf.

Dublin Zoo has always prided itself on its breeding programme and cooperates with zoos worldwide in the conservation of endangered species. Lion breeding began in 1857, and 670 lions have been born here, including the lion that roars at the start of MGM movies.

Education is another aspect of the zoo's work: visitors will find skulls, skins, eggs and other objects at the Discovery Centre. Kids also enjoy the City Farm and the Nakuru Safari Train that runs daily in summer and at weekends in winter from the African Plains.

Kilmainham Gaol ❸

Inchicore Rd, Kilmainham, Dublin 8. *Tel* 453 5984. ▦ 51B, 78A, 79. ⭘ Apr–Sep: 9:30am–5pm daily; Oct–Mar: 9:30am–4pm Mon–Sat, 10am–5pm Sun (last adm 1hr before closing). ⬤ 25–26 Dec. 🖼🏠🖥 www.heritageireland.ie

A long tree-lined avenue runs from the Royal Hospital Kilmainham to the grim, grey bulk of Kilmainham Gaol. The building dates from 1796, but was restored in the 1960s. From the 1790s to the mid-19th century, Kilmainham was used as a transportation depot for prisoners bound for Australia.

During its 130 years as a prison, Kilmainham housed many of those involved in the fight for Irish independence, including Robert Emmet *(see p16)* and Charles Stewart Parnell *(p17)*. The last prisoner held during the Civil War was Eamon de Valera *(p18)*, the future President of Ireland, who was released on 16 July 1924, just prior to the gaol's closure.

The tour of the Gaol starts in the chapel, where Joseph Plunkett married Grace Gifford just a few hours before he faced the firing squad for his part in the 1916 Rising *(see p17)*. The tour ends in the prison yard where Plunkett's badly wounded colleague James Connolly, unable to stand up, was strapped into a chair before being shot. It also passes the dank cells of those involved in the 1798, 1803, 1848 and 1867 uprisings, as well as a hard-labour yard. Of the 16 executions that took place in the few days following the Easter Rising, 14 were carried out here. There is a video presentation, and in the exhibition space are pieces depicting various events which took place in the gaol until it finally closed in 1924. There are also personal mementoes of some of the former inmates.

Doorway and gates of the historic Kilmainham Gaol

Tasting a pint of Guinness at a local pub

Guinness Storehouse ❹

St James's Gate, Dublin 8. **Tel** *408 4800.* ▦ *51B, 78A, 123.* ◯ *9:30am–5pm daily (8pm Jul–Aug).* ◕ *Good Fri, 24–26 Dec & 1 Jan.* 🅿 ♿ ▯ ▯
www.guinness-storehouse.com

The Guinness Storehouse is a new development based in St James's Gate Brewery, the original house of Guinness, now completely remodelled. This 1904 listed building covers nearly four acres of floor space over six floors built around a huge pint glass atrium. The first impression the visitor has is of walking into a large glass pint with light spilling down from above and a copy of the original lease signed by Arthur Guinness enshrined on the floor. The Ingredients section is next where visitors can touch, smell and feel the ingredients through interactive displays. The tour continues into an authentic Georgian anteroom to 'meet' Arthur Guinness and see him at work. The Brewing Process is a noisy, steamy and 'hoppy' area giving the impression of brewing all around with full explanation of the process. The historical development of Guinness cooperage is accompanied by video footage of the craft. Models and displays tell the story of Guinness's transportation, the appeal of Guinness worldwide, and their popular advertising campaigns. The tour ends with a generous tasting of draught Guinness, either in the traditional Brewery Bar or the rooftop Gravity Bar with 360-degree views across Dublin.

The Brewing of Guinness

Label from a Guinness bottle

Guinness is a black beer, known as "stout", renowned for its distinctive malty flavour and smooth, creamy head. From its humble beginnings over 200 years ago, the Guinness brewery site at St James's Gate now covers 26 ha (65 acres) and has its own water and electricity supply. It is the largest brewery in Europe and exports beers to more than 120 countries. Other brands owned by Guinness include Harp Lager and Smithwick's Ale.

HOW GUINNESS IS MADE

The four main ingredients used to brew Guinness are barley, hops, yeast and water which, contrary to popular belief, comes from the Wicklow Mountains rather than the River Liffey.

Barley

Flaked barley

Malted barley

Roasted barley

Water

Masher

Grist

Grist mill

Kieve

1 Irish barley is prepared in three ways – malted, flaked and roasted (to give the distinctive tint). These are all ground together in a grist mill to form a grist.

2 The grist is mixed together with hot water and mashed into a porridge-like consistency. The mixture is strained into a kieve, or mash tun, and left to stand. Here starches are turned into sugars, producing a dark, sweet wort, or an infusion of malt.

Sweet wort

Residual husks are removed

Guinness advertising *has become almost as famous as the product itself. Since 1929, when the first advertisement announced that "Guinness is Good for You", poster and television advertising campaigns have employed many amusing images of both animals and people.*

ARTHUR GUINNESS

In December 1759, 34-year-old Arthur Guinness signed a 9,000-year lease at an annual rent of £45 to take over St James's Gate Brewery, which had lain vacant for almost ten years. At the time the brewing industry in Dublin was at a low ebb – the standard of ale was much criticized and in rural Ireland beer was virtually unknown, as whiskey, gin and poteen were the more favoured drinks. Furthermore, Irish beer was under threat from imports. Guinness started brewing ale, but was also aware of a black ale called porter, produced in London. This new beer was so called because of its popularity with porters at Billingsgate and Covent Garden markets. Guinness decided to stop making ales and develop his own recipe for porter (the word "stout" was not used until the 1920s). So successful was the switch that he made his first export shipment in 1769.

Arthur Guinness

Engraving (c. 1794) of a satisfied customer

Hops

Yeast

5 The liquid has now become a stout. The Guinness is matured and conditioned for up to ten days in tall storage tanks. It is then pumped into tankers or kegs to be sold throughout the world.

Stainless steel kegs

Kettle

Hopped wort

Stout

3 Hops, which provide the tangy taste in Guinness, are added to the wort in huge 20-tonne kettles. The ingredients are boiled to very high temperatures for about 90 minutes and then strained.

Centrifuge

4 The hopped wort is cooled and the yeast is added. The mixture is passed to a fermenting vessel where some sugars are turned to alcohol. It is left to ferment for 48 hours and the yeast is removed by centrifuge.

Draught and bottled Guinness

The Guinness brewery *has relied heavily on water transport since its first export was shipped to England in 1769. The barges which, up until 1961, made the short trip with their cargo down the Liffey to Dublin Port, were a familiar sight on the river. Once at port, the stout would be loaded on to huge tanker ships for worldwide distribution.*

Steel kettles used in modern-day brewing

The elegant façade of the Royal Hospital Kilmainham

Irish Musem of Modern Art – Royal Hospital Kilmainham ❺

Kilmainham, Dublin 8. *Tel* 612 9900.
🚉 *Heuston Station.* 🚌 *26, 51, 51B, 78A, 79, 90, 123.* **Irish Museum of Modern Art** ⬜ *10am–5:30pm Tue, Thu–Sat; 10:30am–5:30pm Wed; noon–5:30pm Sun & public hols (last adm: 5:15pm).* ⬤ *Good Fri, 24–26, 30 Dec.* 📷 🖥 🏠 ♿ *limited.* **www**.imma.ie

Ireland's finest surviving 17th-century building was laid out in 1680, and styled on Les Invalides in Paris. It was built by Sir William Robinson, who also built Marsh's Library *(see p61)*, as a home for 300 wounded soldiers, rather than as a hospital as its name suggests. It retained this role until 1927 and was the first such institution in the British Isles, erected even before the Chelsea Hospital in London. When it was completed, people were so impressed by its elegant Classical symmetry that it was suggested it would be better used as the main campus of Trinity College. The building's design is functional, but the Baroque chapel has fine wood carvings and intricate heraldic stained glass. The plaster ceiling is a replica of the original, which fell down in 1902.

In 1991, the hospital's former residential quarters were imaginatively converted to house the **Irish Museum of Modern Art**. The collection includes a cross-section of Irish and international modern and contemporary art. Works are displayed on a rotating basis and include group and solo shows, retrospectives and special visiting exhibitions.

National Museum at Collins Barracks ❻

See pp86–7.

Shaw's Birthplace ❼

33 Synge St, Dublin 8. *Tel* 475 0854.
🚌 *16, 19, 22.* ⬜ *May–Sep: 10am–1pm & 2–5pm Mon–Fri, 2–5pm Sat, Sun & public hols (groups by arrangement).* ⬤ *Wed.* 📷 🖥 🏠 **www**.visitdublin.com

Playwright and Nobel prize-winner George Bernard Shaw was born in this Victorian house on 26 July 1856. In 1876 he followed his mother to London. She had left four years earlier with her daughters, fed

The recreated Victorian kitchen in Shaw's Birthplace

up with her husband's drinking habits. In London, Shaw met his wife-to-be Charlotte Payne-Townsend. He never returned to Dublin, remaining in England until his death.

Inside the house, visitors can see the young Shaw's bedroom and the kitchen where the author drank "much tea out of brown delft left to 'draw' on the hob until it was pure tannin". Also on view are the nursery, the maid's room and the drawing room, all furnished in period style.

Although there is little in the museum on Shaw's productive years, the house does give an interesting insight into the lives of a typical middle-class Victorian family.

GEORGE BERNARD SHAW

Born in Dublin in 1856, Shaw moved to England at the age of 20 where he began his literary career somewhat unsuccessfully as a critic and novelist. It was not until his first play was produced in 1892 that his career finally took off. One of the most prolific writers of his time, Shaw's many works include *Heartbreak House, Man and Superman*, and, perhaps most famously, *Pygmalion*, which was later adapted into the successful musical *My Fair Lady*. He often attacked conventional thinking and was a supporter of many causes, including vegetarianism and feminism. He lived an abstemious life and died in 1950 at the age of 94.

Ballsbridge ❽

Co Dublin. 🚌 5,7, 7A, 8, 18, 45.

Laid out mostly between 1830 and 1860, the suburb of Ballsbridge is a very exclusive part of Dublin, attracting many wealthy residents. Many of the streets are named after military heroes. Running off Pembroke Road the elegant tree-lined streets such as Raglan Road and Wellington Road are lined with prestigious red-brick houses. The area is also home to several foreign embassies – look for the striking cylindrical US Embassy building at the junction of Northumberland and Eglin roads – as well as a number of upmarket hotels and guesthouses.

Close to Baggot Street Bridge is a statue of the poet Patrick Kavanagh, depicted reclining on a bench. This attractive stretch of the Grand Canal at Lower Baggot Street was one of the poet's favourite parts of Dublin.

The southeast sector of Ballsbridge, just across the River Dodder, is dominated by the Royal Dublin Society Showgrounds (often simply abbreviated to RDS). Founded in 1731 to promote science, the arts and agriculture, the Royal Dublin Society was an instrumental mover behind the creation of most of Ireland's national museums

Late 18th-century engraving of a passenger ferry passing Harcourt Lock on the Grand Canal, taken from a painting by James Barralet

DUBLIN'S CANALS

The affluent Georgian era witnessed the building of the Grand and Royal canals linking Dublin with the River Shannon and the west coast. These two canals became the main arteries of trade and public transport in Ireland from the 1760s until the coming of the railways, which took much of the passenger business, almost a century later. However, the canals continued to carry freight until after World War II, finally closing to commercial traffic in 1960. Today the canals are well maintained and used mainly for pleasure-boating, cruising and fishing.

and galleries. The two major events at the sprawling yet graceful showgrounds are the Spring Show in May and the Horse Show in August (see p27). Throughout the rest of the year the showground plays host to various conventions, exhibitions and concerts.

The Lansdowne Road stadium, the home of the Irish national rugby and soccer teams, is another Ballsbridge landmark. Supporters in the teams' orange, green and white colours can often be seen in the area.

Stretch of the Grand Canal near the Waterways Visitors' Centre

Waterways Visitors' Centre ❾

Grand Canal Quay, Dublin 2. **Tel** 677 7510. 🚉 DART to Grand Canal Dock. 🚌 2, 3. ☐ Jun–Sep: 9:30am–5:30pm daily; Oct–May: 12:30–5pm Wed–Sun. ⬤ 25 Dec. 📷 📹 on request. **www**.waterwaysireland.com

Fifteen minutes' walk from Trinity College along Pearse Street, the Waterways Visitors' Centre overlooks the Grand Canal Basin. Audiovisual displays and models illustrate the history of Ireland's inland waterways. One of the most interesting focuses on their construction: in the 1700s, canals were often called "navigations" and the men who built them were "navigators", a term shortened to "navvies". There are also exhibits on the wildlife found in the canals and surrounding marshlands.

The Royal Dublin Showground at Ballsbridge

The National Museum at Collins Barracks ❻

Commissioned by William III in 1700, this was the largest barracks in his domain, with living accommodation for over 5,000 soldiers. Originally known as Dublin Barracks, it was renamed Collins Barracks after Michael Collins *(see p18)* following Irish independence. This decorative arts annexe of the National Museum *(see pp44–5)* displays the fine exhibits, from furniture to silver, by making full use of up-to-date technology including a multimedia catalogue and clever lighting. Currently occupying only two blocks, the museum is planned to extend eventually to fill all four wings.

Silver coffee pot

Scientific Instruments
The fascinating display of surveying and navigation instruments includes this astrolabe (c.1580–90), which was made in Prague by Erasmus Habermel.

South block

Entrance

Ground floor

★ Irish Silver
This silver-gilt bowl by Thomas Bolton dates from 1703. Also known as a monteith, it was used for cooling wine glasses.

Skinners Alley Chair
Dating back to c.1730, this impressive gilt chair is part of the museum's collection of Irish period furniture. It was made for the Protestant aldermen of the Corporation of Skinners Alley, who were removed from the Dublin Assembly by James II. The society was eventually incorporated into the Orange Order.

STAR EXHIBITS

- ★ William Smith O'Brien Gold Cup
- ★ Irish Silver
- ★ The Fonthill Vase

Third floor

Second floor

★ The Fonthill Vase
This beautiful 14th-century Chinese vase takes its name from Fonthill Abbey, near Salisbury in England, one of its many homes before it came to this museum.

VISITORS' CHECKLIST

Benburb Street, Dublin 7.
Tel 677 7444. 🚌 25, 25A, 66, 67, 90. ⬤ 10am–5pm Tue–Sat, 2–5pm Sun.
⬤ Good Fri, 25 Dec. 📷 ♿
🅿 🚫 www.museum.ie

★ William Smith O'Brien Gold Cup
After an uprising in 1848, O'Brien was sent to Australia and imprisoned. On his release he was presented with this 22-carat gold cup by his supporters in Australia.

Military History Wing
This space includes The History of the Irish Soldier (1550–2001) and the Stokes Tapestry (below).

First floor

West block

Main entrance

North block

Military History Wing

GALLERY GUIDE
Furniture, silver and scientific instrument collections are in the south block. In the west block exhibits include musical instruments, glass, clothing and jewellery. The Curators' Choice section displays 25 objects, individually chosen by the curators of the museum for their cultural significance.

KEY TO FLOORPLAN

- ☐ Irish Country Furniture
- ☐ The Way We Wore
- ☐ Eileen Gray
- ☐ Period Furniture
- ☐ Scientific Instruments
- ☐ Out of Storage
- ☐ Exhibition Development
- ☐ Irish Silver
- ☐ Curators' Choice
- ☐ Origin of National Collections
- ☐ Temporary exhibitions
- ☐ Military History Wing
- ☐ Non-exhibition space

Marino Casino ⑩

Cherrymount Crescent, off Malahide
Rd. **Tel** 833 1618. 🚆 DART to
Clontarf. 🚌 20A, 20B, 27A, 27B, 42,
42C, 123 IMP. ◯ Nov–Apr: 10am–
6pm Mon–Fri, noon–4pm Sat, Sun
& public hols; May, Oct: 10am–5pm
daily; Jun–Sep: 10am–6pm daily. For
group bookings outside these times,
call 833 1618. 🖼 🎥 obligatory
(last tour: 45 mins before closing).
www.heritageireland.ie

This delightful little villa,
designed by Sir William
Chambers in the 1760s for
Lord Charlemont, now sits
next to a busy road.
Originally built as
a summer house
for the Marino
Estate, the villa
survives today
although the main
house was pulled down
in 1921. The Casino is one of
the finest examples of Neo-
Classical architecture in Ireland.
Some innovative features
were used in its construction,
including chimneys disguised
as urns and hollow columns
that accommodate drains.

Outside, four fine carved stone
lions stand guard at each of the
corners. The building's squat,
compact exterior conceals 16
rooms arranged on three floors
around a central staircase. The
ground floor comprises a spacious hall and a saloon, with
beautiful silk hangings. On the
first floor is the state bedroom.

State bedroom

The saloon, the Casino's
main room, was used for
formal entertaining.

The basement contains the
servants' hall, the
kitchen, pantry and wine cellar.

Entrance

The hall ends in a
semi-circular apse
leading to the saloon.

Spectacular giant water lilies in the Lily
House, National Botanic Gardens

National Botanic Gardens ⑪

Botanic Ave, Glasnevin, Dublin 9.
Tel 857 0909. 🚌 13, 19, 19A, 83,
134. ◯ Apr–Oct: 9am–6pm daily;
Nov–Mar: 9am–4:30pm daily.
⬤ 25 Dec. 🖥 ♿ 🎥 free Sun at
2:30pm. **www**.botanicgardens.ie

Opened in 1795, these
gardens are home to Ireland's
foremost centre of botany
and horticulture. They still
possess an old-world
feel, thanks to the
beautiful cast-iron
Palm House and
other curvilinear
glasshouses. These
were built between
1843 and 1869 by
Richard Turner, who
was also responsible
for the Palm House at
Kew Gardens, Lon-
don, and the glass-
houses in Belfast's
Botanic Gardens.
The 20-ha (48-acre)
park contains over
16,000 different plant species.
A particularly attractive feature is the colourful display
of Victorian carpet bedding.
Other highlights include a
renowned rose garden and
rich collections of cacti and
orchids. Pampas grass and
the giant lily were first grown
in Europe here.
    One path, known as Yew
Walk, has trees that date back
to the early 18th century and
there is also a giant redwood
that towers to 30 m (100 ft).

Glasnevin Cemetery ⑫

Finglas Rd, Glasnevin. **Tel** 830 1133.
🚌 40, 40A, 40B from Parnell St,
40C. ◯ 8am–4:30pm daily.

Originally known as Prospect
Cemetery, this is Ireland's
largest graveyard, with

Impressive gravestones in
Glasnevin Cemetery

approximately 1.2 million people buried here. It was established by Daniel O'Connell in 1832 and was viewed as a great achievement on his part, since Catholics were previously unable to conduct graveside ceremonies because of the Penal Laws.

O'Connell's endeavours have been rewarded with the most conspicuous monument – a 51-m (167-ft) tall round-tower in the early Irish Christian style stands over his crypt.

While the maze of head-stones exhibits a tremendous variety of designs, none, apart from O'Connell's, has been allowed by the cemetery's committee to be too resplen-dent. However the graves conjure up a very Irish feel with high crosses and insignia such as shamrocks, harps and Irish wolfhounds.

The most interesting sector is the oldest part by Prospect Square, on the far right-hand side. Look for the two watch-towers built into the medieval-looking walls. These were erected as lookouts for the bodysnatchers hired by 19th-century surgeons. Before the Anatomy Act permitted corpses to be donated to science, this was the only way medical students could learn. Staff at the cemetery office will gladly give directions to graves of famous people such as Charles Stewart Parnell, Eamon De Valera, Michael Collins and Brendan Behan. A small Republican plot holds the remains of Countess Constance Markievicz and Maud Gonne MacBride, while the body of poet Gerard Manley Hopkins lies in the Jesuit Plot.

Glasnevin also reveals some interesting landscaping; the paths that run between the plots follow the same routes as the original woodland trails. Copses of mature syca-more and oak have been maintained while some of the more interesting imports among the thousand trees to be found here include a Californian Giant Sequoia and a Cedar of Lebanon.

The oak-beamed Great Hall at Malahide Castle

Malahide Castle ⑬

Malahide, Co Dublin. 🚉 🚌 42. **Tel** 846 2184. ☐ Apr–Sep: 10am–5pm Mon–Sat, 10am–6pm Sun, public hols; Oct–Mar: 10am– 5pm Mon–Sat, 11am–5pm Sun, public hols. 🖼 ▣ 🎫 last tours 4:30pm. **www**.visitdublin.com

Near the seaside dormitory town of Malahide stands a huge castle set in 100 ha (250 acres) of grounds. The castle's core dates from the 14th century but later additions, such as its rounded towers, have given it a classic fairy-tale appearance. Originally a fortress, the building served as a stately home for the Talbot family until 1973. They were staunch supporters of James II: the story goes that, on the day of the Battle of the Boyne in 1690 (*see p15*), 14 members of the family breakfasted here; none came back for supper.

Candelabra at Malahide Castle

Guided tours take in the impressive oak-beamed Great Hall, the Oak Room with its carved panelling, and the castle's collection of 18th-century Irish furniture. Part of the Portrait Collection, on loan from the National Gallery (*see pp48–51*), can be seen here. It includes portraits of the Talbot family, and other figures such as Wolfe Tone (*see p16*).

Fry Model Railway Museum ⑭

Malahide Castle grounds, Malahide, Co Dublin. **Tel** 846 3779. 🚌 42 from Beresford Place, near Busáras. 🚉 and DART to Malahide. ☐ Apr–Sep: 10am–1pm, 2–5pm Sat–Thu, 2–6pm Sun, public hols. 🌑 Fri & Oct–Mar. 🖼 ♿ **www**.visitdublin.com

Set in the grounds of Mala-hide Castle, this collection of handmade models of Irish trains and trams was started by Cyril Fry, a railway engin-eer and draughtsman, in the 1920s. It is one of the largest such displays in the world. Running on a 32-mm wide (0-gauge) track, each detailed piece is made to scale and journeys through a landscape featuring the major Dublin landmarks, including the River Liffey complete with model barges. As well as his-toric trains, there are also models of the DART line, trains, buses and ferries.

A smaller room exhibits static displays of memorabilia and larger-scale models.

Howth ⓯

Co Dublin. ▣ *DART.* **Howth Castle grounds** ◯ *8am–sunset daily.*

The commercial fishing town of Howth marks the northern limit of Dublin Bay. Before Dun Laoghaire, or Kingstown as it was known then, took over, Howth was the main harbour for Dublin.

Howth Head, a huge rocky mass, has lovely views of the bay. A footpath runs around the tip of Howth Head, which is known locally as the "Nose". Nearby is Baily Lighthouse (1814). Sadly, much of this area – some of Ireland's prime real estate – has suffered from building development.

To the west of the town is Howth Castle, which dates back to Norman times. Its grounds are particularly beautiful in May and June when the rhododendrons and azaleas are in full bloom. The National Transport Museum in the grounds is worth a visit.

Ireland's Eye, an islet and bird sanctuary where puffins nest, can be reached by a short boat trip from Howth.

Yachts anchored in Dun Laoghaire harbour

Dun Laoghaire ⓰

Co Dublin. ▣ *DART.* **National Maritime Museum** *Tel* 280 0969. **Comhaltas Ceoltóiri Éireann** *Tel* 280 0295. ◯ *music Tue, Wed, Fri & Sat nights, céilis Fri.* ▣ ▣ ▣ **Lambert Puppet Theatre** *Tel* 280 0974. ◯ *for performances Sat & Sun 3:30pm.* ▣

Dublin's southern ferry port and yachting centre, with its bright villas, parks and palm trees, makes a surprising introduction to Ireland, usually known for its grey dampness. For a time Dun Laoghaire (pronounced Dunleary) was called Kingstown, after a visit by King George IV of England in 1821. Its original name was restored under the Free State in 1921, though the building of a rail line to Dublin in 1834 resulted in the demolition of the original *dún* or fort after which it is named.

Many visitors arriving on the ferry head straight for Dublin or the countryside. However, the town offers some magnificent walks around the harbour and to the lighthouse along the east pier. The pretty **People's Park** at the end of George's Street has a coffee shop and hosts a flower show on the second weekend in August, while the outlying villages of Sandycove and Dalkey can be reached via "The Metals"; a footpath that runs alongside the railway line.

In the Mariners' Church is the **National Maritime Museum**, now under renovation. Exhibits include a longboat used by French officers during Wolfe Tone's unsuccessful invasion at Bantry in 1796.

Just up the road (or DART line) in Monkstown's Belgrave Square, is the **Comhaltas Ceoltóiri Éireann**, Ireland's main centre for traditional music and dancing, with regular music sessions and *ceilís* (dances). Nearby, the **Lambert Puppet Theatre** on Clifton Lane offers classic pantomime fun for kids by the creators of beloved children's TV show *Wanderly Wagon*.

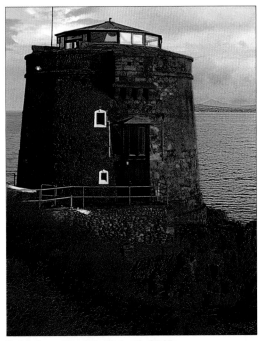

Martello Tower at Howth Head just north of Dublin

James Joyce Tower ⑰

Sandycove, Co Dublin. **Tel** 280 9265.
🚊 DART to Sandycove. ⭘ Mar–Oct:
10am–5pm Mon–Sat, 2–6pm Sun,
public hols. ● 1–2pm weekdays. ▨

Standing on a rocky promontory above the village of Sandycove is this Martello tower. It is one of 15 defensive towers which were erected between Dublin and Bray in 1804 to withstand a threatened invasion by Napoleon. They were named after a tower on Cape Mortella in Corsica. One hundred years later James Joyce *(see p23)* stayed in this tower for a week as the guest of Oliver St John Gogarty, poet and model for the *Ulysses* character Buck Mulligan. Gogarty rented the tower for a mere £8 per year. Today, inside the squat 12-m (40-ft) tower's granite walls is a small museum with some of Joyce's correspondence, personal belongings, such as his guitar, cigar case and walking stick, and his death mask. There are also photographs and several first editions of his works, including a deluxe edition (1935) of *Ulysses* illustrated by Henri Matisse. The roof, originally a gun platform but later used as a sunbathing deck by Gogarty, affords marvellous views across Dublin Bay. Directly below the tower is the Forty Foot Pool, which was traditionally an all-male nude bathing spot, but is now open to both sexes.

Guitar at the museum, James Joyce Tower

Dalkey ⑱

Co Dublin. 🚊 DART.

Dalkey was once known as the "Town of Seven Castles", but only two of these fortified mansions, dating from the 15th and 16th centuries, now remain. They are both on the main street of this attractive village whose tight, winding roads and charming villas give it a Mediterranean feel.

A little way offshore is tiny Dalkey Island, a rocky bird sanctuary with a Martello tower and a medieval Benedictine church, both now in a poor state of repair. In summer the island can be reached by a boat ride from the town's Coliemore Harbour. The island was, at one time, held by Danish pirates. In the 18th century, a Dublin club used to gather on the island to crown a mock "King of Dalkey" and his officers of state. Originally done simply for fun, the ceremony was stopped in 1797 by Lord Clare when it became a political issue. It began again in the late 1970s.

Shopfronts lining the main street of Dalkey village

Killiney ⑲

Co Dublin. 🚊 DART to Dalkey or Killiney.

South of Dalkey, the coastal road climbs uphill before tumbling down into the winding leafy lanes around Killiney village. The route offers one of the most scenic vistas on this stretch of the east coast, with views that are often compared to those across the Bay of Naples in Italy. Howth Head is clearly visible to the north, with Bray Head *(see p116)* and the foothills of the Wicklow Mountains *(see p113)* to the south. There is another exhilarating view from the top of windswept Killiney Hill Park, off Victoria Road. It is well worth tackling the steep trail up from the village to see it. Down below is the popular pebbly beach, Killiney Strand.

View southwards from Killiney Hill over Killiney Bay towards the Wicklow Mountains

THREE GUIDED WALKS

The scale of the city and the lack of many hills make Dublin an ideal place for walking. Many of the tourist attractions and the loveliest Georgian squares are within short distances of each other. The weather can be changeable, but that is a good excuse to drop into a local pub for a drink until the rain clears up.

Draught and bottled Guinness

The following walks give you a sense of three very different faces of the city. You can discover remnants

of the old Viking town around Christ Church Cathedral; follow in the footsteps of Dublin's best-known literary figures; or take a trip to the nearby medieval village of Dalkey. There, you can enjoy great views of Dublin Bay and the beautiful Wicklow Mountains, only a short distance away. In addition to these walks, each of the three areas in the *Area-by-Area* section of the book offers a short walk on its *Street-by-Street* map.

CHOOSING A WALK

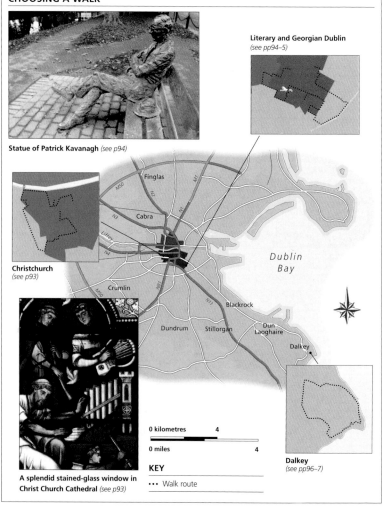

Statue of Patrick Kavanagh *(see p94)*

Literary and Georgian Dublin
(see pp94–5)

Finglas

Cabra

Christchurch
(see p93)

Crumlin

Dublin Bay

Blackrock

Dundrum   Stillorgan   Dun Laoghaire

Dalkey

A splendid stained-glass window in Christ Church Cathedral *(see p93)*

0 kilometres   4

0 miles   4

Dalkey
(see pp96–7)

KEY

••• Walk route

A 45-Minute Walk Around Christchurch

Although every part of Dublin boasts a rich heritage, it is in Christchurch, at the heart of the original Viking town, that the layers of history lie thickest on the ground. Much evidence of the past has sadly been lost through development; however, a few precious hints remain, including sections of the city wall and street names that suggest past uses, stories and personalities.

The bridge to the Synod Hall, part of Christ Church Cathedral ⑦

Begin at the grand entrance to **City Hall** ① *(see p55)* and head up Parliament Street towards the Liffey. You will pass an old sign for **Thomas Reade's Cutlers** ②, a 17th-century sword shop. Turn left into **Essex Gate** ③, one of the old entrances into the town. If you look through the ground-level bar grille of the corner building on Exchange Street, it is possible to see the base of **Isolde's Tower** ④, part of the 13th-century Anglo-Norman wall. Go down Essex Street West and stop for a coffee at **Cultivate** ⑤. Continue to Fishamble Street ⑥, named after the fish market that was located here in medieval times.

Cross over to John's Lane East, behind the spectacularly imposing **Christ Church Cathedral** ⑦ *(see pp64–5)*, Ireland's oldest cathedral. Viewing windows allow you to admire a section of the Hiberno-Norse town wall, located in the basement of the **Civic Offices** ⑧.

Head up Winetavern Street, on to Merchant's Quay and pause at **Father Matthew Bridge** ⑨, site of the original ford over the Liffey where the city was founded. Stop for a drink at the **Brazen Head** ⑩ *(see p146)*, the city's oldest pub. Turn left onto Cook Street and cross the grounds of **St Audoen's Church** ⑪ *(see pp62–3)* via its famous arch, the last remaining gateway of the old city. Turn right and follow Thomas Street West

until the crossroads with St Augustine Street. This former Gaelic crossing point pre-dates the Vikings. Go down **Francis Street** ⑫, lined with a number of attractive antiques shops. Turn left towards **St Patrick's Cathedral** ⑬ *(see p61)*, Ireland's largest church. Cross the grounds to Golden Lane and turn left onto Ship Street Great, behind ancient **Dublin Castle** ⑭ *(see pp56–7)*. Follow Ship

Street Little to **St Werburgh's Church** ⑮ *(see p62)*, and back on to Christchurch Place where you can catch a bus to various points across the city.

KEY

••• Walk route

TIPS FOR WALKERS

Starting point: *City Hall.*
Length: *2.5 km (1.5 miles).*
Getting there: *Buses 49X, 50, 50X, 51B, 77X, 78A, 123 and 206 to Christchurch Place.*
Stopping-off points: *Cultivate for a Fairtrade coffee; the Brazen Head for a pint or Guinness stew; and Leo Burdock's (see p141) for the best fish 'n' chips in Dublin.*

The sign for Thomas Reade's Cutlers, a 17th-century sword shop ②

A 90-Minute Walk Through Literary And Georgian Dublin

Dublin has an enviable literary heritage and, as a result, there are endless routes one could take to follow in the footsteps of world-famous poets, dramatists and novelists. The walk detailed below passes through some of the city's loveliest Georgian squares and parks and along an attractive section of the Grand Canal, finishing up where many Irish writers got their inspiration – their local pubs.

Trinity to the Grand Canal
Begin at **Trinity College** ① *(see pp38–40)*, alma mater to Jonathan Swift *(see p61)*, author of the world-famous *Gulliver's Travels*; JM Synge, a renowned Irish dramatist; and Nobel Prize-winning playwright Samuel Beckett *(see p23)*, best known for *Waiting for Godot*. Walk east from the Lincoln Place entrance, passing Westland Row, where the prolific literary genius Oscar Wilde *(see p23)* was born. At the corner of Lincoln Place is **Sweeny's Chemist** ②, where Leopold Bloom, the protagonist of James Joyce's masterpiece *Ulysses (see p23)*, would buy lemon soap. Head to Merrion Square. As a child, Wilde lived at **No. 1** ③, and it was on this corner that Joyce was stood up on a first date by his future wife, Nora Barnacle. Continue to the reclining **Wilde Statue** ④ and then to the plaques on the square's south side, commemorating the celebrated poet WB Yeats, who lived at **No. 82** ⑤; influential Irish writer AE

Russell worked at **No. 84** ⑥; and Joseph Le Fanu, a Gothic writer who impressed both Bram Stoker *(see p22)* and Joyce, lived at **No. 70** ⑦. On the corner of Mount Street Upper is **Number 29** ⑧ *(see p47)*, a re-creation of a Georgian house. Continue to **St Stephen's Church** ⑨. Pass Herbert Street, on your right, where the successful Irish dramatist Brendan Behan lived in the 1950s. The Grand Canal is ahead. Turn right, following the path by the water.

Grand Canal to the RHA
On Herbert Place is a plaque to novelist Elizabeth Bowen, born at **No. 15** ⑩ in 1899. As a boy, Flann O'Brien (aka Brian O'Nolan), author of *The Third Policeman*, lived at **No. 25** ⑪. Continue along the canal to the **Statue of Patrick Kavanagh** ⑫. This immensely popular poet often referred to the canal and nearby streets in his works. Turn up Cumberland Road to **Fitzwilliam Square** ⑬. In the 1930s, WB Yeats lived at No. 42. Exit the square, returning to Fitzwilliam Street, and continue to Baggot Street Lower. At No. 3 is the

KEY
••• Walk route

Pretty Georgian terrace houses lining Fitzwilliam Square ⑬

United Arts Club ⑭, founded in 1907 by WB Yeats and AE Russell among others to promote writing, visual art and music. Continue down Baggot Street to **Toner's Pub** ⑮, the only Dublin bar Yeats ever had a drink in. At the next crossroads, you come to **Ely Place** ⑯ (*see p42*). Oscar Wilde proposed to Constance Lloyd at No. 1, while surgeon and writer Oliver St John Go- garty lived at what is now the Royal Hibernian Academy (*see p47*).

Plaque for Bram Stoker

St Stephen's Green to the Carmelite Church

Continue on Merrion Row to St Stephen's Green, past the 17th-century **Huguenot Cemetery** ⑰ (closed to visitors) and the **Shelbourne Hotel** ⑱ (*see p130*).

Among the writers who lived on or around **St Stephen's Green** ⑲ (*see p41*) are the 19th-century poet James Clarence Mangan; 19th-century Gothic writer Charles Maturin; and James Stephens, poet and writer of fairy tales. Gothic master Bram Stoker was born at No. 30 Kildare Street, just off the green to the right. Cross the green to emerge at **Newman House** ⑳ (*see p42*) to the south. Poet Gerard Manley Hopkins lived and taught here. You can see his room and the classroom of James Joyce, who studied here when it was part of University College Dublin. Continue round the green, taking a left at York Street. Walk to the **Whitefriar Street Carmelite Church** ㉑ (*see p60*).

The façade of the grand Shelbourne Hotel on St Stephen's Green ⑱

Ghosts, pubs and old books

Also on Aungier Street is the birthplace of poet Thomas Moore at No. 12, now a pub. Joseph Le Fanu based some ghost stories around here, too.

Take a right on to Stephen Street Lower for Chatham Street, and visit **McDaid's** ㉒, Brendan Behan's local pub; he and Patrick Kavanagh were never allowed in at the same time to avoid fisticuffs. Turn left into Grafton Street and right to Duke Street. More refreshment awaits in three famous pubs: **Davy Byrne's** ㉓, the setting for a famous scene in *Ulysses*, and **The Duke** ㉔ and **The Bailey** ㉕, both fre- quented by Brendan Behan, Patrick Kavanagh, Flann O'Brien, James Joyce among others. Finally, go into **Cathach Books** ㉖ to browse through rare editions of old favourites. Catch a bus from Nassau Street.

Pearse Street

MERRION SQ N

MERRION SQUARE

MERRION SQ E

MERRION SQ N

MERRION SQ SOUTH

MOUNT ST UPPER

FITZWILLIAM LANE

FITZWILLIAM ST LOWER

FITZWILLIAM ST UPPER

JAMES'S STREET EAST

BAGGOT STREET LOWER

BAGGOT STREET UPPER

GGOT STREET LOWER

BROKE STREET LR

ZWILLIAM SQ N

ZWILLIAM SQUARE

LAD LANE

WILTON PLACE

HERBERT STREET

HERBERT LANE

HERBERT PLACE

PERCY PLACE

WILTON TERRACE

CUMBERLAND RD

MESPIL ROAD

0 metres   300

0 yards   300

TIPS FOR WALKERS

Starting point: *Lincoln Gate, Trinity College.*
Length: *2.5 km (1.5 miles).*
Getting there: *DART to Pearse Street; a huge number of buses serve the area around Trinity. Stopping along Nassau Street are 4, 5, 7, 7A/B/C/D, 8, 10, 11, 11A/B, 14, 14A, 46A/B/C/D/E, 63, 74, 92, 116, 117, 118, 145.*
Stopping-off points: *There are several pleasant eateries near Baggot Street Bridge, or you can have lunch on La Peniche barge restaurant (see p139), near the Kavanagh statue, on the Grand Canal. Ely Winebar (see p139) is on Ely Place, and there are many pubs along the route for drinks.*

The tranquil surroundings of the Grand Canal

A 90-Minute Walk Around Dalkey

The picturesque village of Dalkey *(see p91)* has a fascinating history and stunning coastal views. In medieval times, it was Dublin's main deep-water port, and it thrived on maritime trade until the 1600s, when Dublin itself became a safe port for shipping. Dalkey then declined into a sleepy fishing village. Its fortunes turned once again in the 19th century, with the decision to build a protective pier at nearby Dún Laoghaire. Granite for the pier was quarried in Dalkey, bringing the town into the limelight once more. This walk goes along winding streets and past homely cottages snuggling up to grand mansions, now home to the rich and famous.

Roseate tern from a colony breeding off Dalkey Island

Castle Street to Coliemore Harbour and Dillon's Park

Start at the **Tramyard** ① on Castle Street, a short stroll from the Dart station. This is where trams from Dublin used to be parked for the night and the horses stabled. The last tram ran from Dublin to Dalkey in 1949.

The former site of most of Dalkey's seven medieval castles, **Castle Street** ② now boasts the only two surviving fortified mansions. Walk to the crossroads, turn left down Convent Road and take the first right into Coliemore Road. From here, you will catch tantalizing glimpses of the sea and Dalkey Island in-between colourful gardens, quirky cottages and grand mansions. Pass the fairy-tale **Cliff Castle** ③, a famous hotel in the 1920s and now the Moroccan embassy. Further along is **Inniscorrig** ④, a mansion once owned by Dominic Corrigan, a physician who brought running water to Dalkey. If the gate is open, you will see his face carved above the doorway.

At **Coliemore Harbour** ⑤, home to lobster fishermen, you will get a better view of Dalkey Island. Named after its shape (its Gaelic name, *Deilg Inis*, means "Thorn Island"), the island has been inhabited since 4,500 BC; these days only goats live there. On the island are the ruins of a 9th-century church and a Martello tower, one of 26 built between Dublin and Bray as defence posts against a Napoleonic invasion that never came. Note the outlying rocks, Lamb Island and Maiden Rock, which was named after some local girls who drowned while collecting shellfish. These are now a

Pretty Coliemore Harbour ④, with a clear view of Dalkey Island

TIPS FOR WALKERS

Starting point: *Castle Street.*
Length: *2.5 km (1.5 miles).*
Getting there: *30 minutes by DART south from the city centre; buses number 8 (very infrequent) and 59 from Dún Laoghaire.*
Stopping-off points: *There are high-quality restaurants and cafés all along Castle Street. On Coliemore Road is Nosh (see p144).*

breeding ground for a rare species of roseate tern.

Continue to **Dillon's Park** ⑥. A Mrs Dillon operated tea rooms here in Victorian times. Take a rest, and enjoy the clear view of Dalkey Island.

Famous residents
Walk a little further and take the steps on the right up to **Sorrento Park** ⑦. Follow the path past a rock face with a mosaic of John Dowland, an Elizabethan poet said to have been born in Dalkey, who was a friend of William

Goats roaming on Dalkey Island

to the ultra-wealthy. Further up the road, opposite a house called Strawberry Hill, the high wall on your right will break for zigzagging steps. Known as the **Cat's Ladder** ⑩, this is the hardest climb of the walk, but there are low walls for rest stops en route. At the top, turn right into Torca Road. A short way up on the left is **Torca Cottage** ⑪, the childhood home of renowned author/playwright George Bernard Shaw. The road eventually turns into Ardbrugh Road. On your left is **Dalkey Quarry** ⑫, which supplied the granite used for the piers of nearby Dún Laoghaire Harbour. Just

before the road forks, a grassy slope down a steep hill appears on your right, separated from the road by bollards. This was the route of the funicular railway that serviced the quarry, and is marked by flagstones. Head down this hill and turn right onto Dalkey Avenue, then stop at the corner of Old Quarry and Summerfield House. Within the grounds of Summerfield House was **Clifton School** ⑬, which features in James Joyce's masterpiece *Ulysses*. At the end of Dalkey Avenue turn right, back into Castle Street.

Castles and Queens
On your right is **Archbold's Castle** ⑭, one of the street's two extant medieval mansions. Beside it is the **Church of the Assumption** ⑮. Cardinal Newman, first rector of the Catholic University of Ireland, spent time here while he lived in Dalkey.

Almost opposite is **Dalkey Castle & Heritage Centre** ⑯, in the 14th-century Goats Castle. The centre provides entertaining, in-depth historical and literary walking tours of the area, plus a tour of the castle led by characters in full period dress. Entrance includes access to the 10th-century St Begnet's Church and a Rathdown Slab, one of 28 unique to the area, believed to be a 10th-century Viking burial marker.

End your walk with a drink at **The Queens** ⑰ *(see p145)*, a landmark pub that's been here since 1745. Turn right at the end of Castle Street to return to the DART station.

KEY

••• Walk route

🚉 Dart station

Shakespeare. As the path splits, veer left to reach **Sorrento Point** ⑧. Pause here to enjoy stunning views of Dalkey Island, Killiney Bay and Hill, and the Wicklow Mountains. This panoramic vista is often compared to the views across the Bay of Naples in Italy.

Exit the park and turn right to reach **Vico Road** ⑨, home

The exterior of the 14th-century Goat Castle

Herb garden, Ardgillan Castle ▷

BEYOND DUBLIN

BEYOND DUBLIN

A short way out of central Dublin, the beautiful Irish countryside offers a wealth of pretty villages, dramatic mountains and elegant stately homes to visit. South of Dublin, the coastline down to Dun Laoghaire and beyond, with its dramatic backdrop of the Wicklow Mountains, is stunning. To the north can be found traces of some of the earliest residents in the area – the Celts.

North of Dublin, the fertile Boyne Valley in County Meath was settled during the Stone Age. The remains of ancient sites from this early civilization fill the area and include New-grange, the finest Neolithic tomb in Ireland. In Celtic times, the focus shifted south to the Hill of Tara, the seat of the High Kings of Ireland and the Celts' spiritual and political capital. Tara's heyday was in the 3rd century AD, but it retained its importance until the Norman invasion in the 1100s.

Norman castles, such as the immense fortress at Trim in County Meath, attest to the shifting frontiers around the region of English influence known as the Pale *(see p108)*. By the end of the 16th century, this area

Coracle from the Millmount Museum in Drogheda

incorporated nearly all the counties in the Midlands. The Boyne Valley returned to prominence in 1690, when the Battle of the Boyne ended in a land-mark Protestant victory over the Catholics *(see p15)*.

The area to the south of Dublin had the strongest English influence in all of Ireland. From the 18th century onwards, wealthy Anglo-Irish families were drawn to what they saw as a stable zone, and felt confident enough to build fine mansions like the Palladian masterpieces of Russ-borough, Newbridge and Castletown.

For a refreshing breath of fresh air, stroll along the cliffs at Bray Head, or follow one of the invigorating walking routes in the Wicklow Mountains.

Traditional kitchen in Newbridge House

◁ View towards the sea beyond Ardgillan Castle

Exploring Beyond Dublin

The countryside around Dublin is stunning and offers everything from stately homes to ancient burial sites and dramatic mountains to seaside villages. The Wicklow Mountains have excellent walking territory and are also home to some of the best sights, such as the elegant gardens of Powerscourt House and the monastic complex at Glendalough. The coastal stretch to the south of Dublin towards Bray is particularly scenic.

The lush gardens at Ardgillan Demesne, situated on the coast north of Dublin

SIGHTS AT A GLANCE

Ardgillan Demesne **17**
Avondale House **8**
The Bog of Allen Nature Centre **3**
The Boyne Valley **23**
Bray **15**
Browne's Hill Dolmen **7**
Carlingford **20**
Castletown House pp106–7 **1**
Drogheda **18**
Dundalk **21**
Glendalough **9**
Hill of Tara **26**
Kilbeggan **29**
Kildare **5**
Killruddery House **13**
Mellifont Abbey **22**
Military Road Tour **11**
Monasterboice **19**
Monasterevin **4**
Mount Usher Gardens **10**
Mullingar **28**
Newbridge Demesne **16**
Newgrange pp120–21 **24**
Powerscourt pp114–15 **14**
Robertstown **2**
Russborough House **6**
Slane **25**
Trim **27**
Wicklow Mountains **12**

The extensive gardens at Avondale House

0 kilometres ——— 20
0 miles ——— 10

- Armagh
- Belfast
- **20** CARLINGFORD
- DUNDALK **21**
- N1
- Louth
- N2
- N52
- Castlebellingham
- Ardee
- **L O U T H**
- *Irish Sea*
- **1** **19** MONASTERBOICE
- MELLIFONT ABBEY **22**
- DROGHEDA
- **18**
- SLANE **25**
- **23** **24** NEWGRANGE
- BOYNE VALLEY
- Navan
- **M E A T H**
- **17** ARDGILLAN DEMESNE
- **26** HILL OF TARA
- M1
- Skerries
- R154
- Ashbourne
- N1
- N3
- N2
- **16** NEWBRIDGE DEMESNE
- Kilcock
- Dunboyne
- Malahide
- M4
- Howth
- **1** CASTLETOWN HOUSE
- **DUBLIN**
- *Dublin Bay*
- N7
- Sallins
- **MILITARY ROAD TOUR**
- Dalkey
- N81
- Naas
- **11**
- Enniskerry
- Blessington
- **14**
- **15** BRAY
- **6** POWERSCOURT
- **13** KILLRUDDERY HOUSE
- RUSSBOROUGH HOUSE
- **W I C K L O W**
- **12**
- N11
- N81
- Laragh
- **10** MOUNT USHER GARDENS
- GLENDALOUGH **9**
- Rathdrum
- Wicklow
- Baltinglass
- **W I C K L O W   M O U N T A I N S**
- Rathvilly
- **8** AVONDALE HOUSE
- Avoca
- Aughrim
- R747
- Tinahely
- Arklow
- N11
- Carnew
- Gorey
- **W E X F O R D**
- N80
- Bunclody
- Ferns
- Waterford, Cork

Elegant stuccoed hall and staircase in Castletown House

KEY

▦▦▦	Motorway
▦▦▦	Major road
▬▬▬	Secondary road
┈┈┈	Minor road
▬▬▬	Scenic route
⊶⊶⊶	Main railway
───	Minor railway
▭▭▭	International border
▭▭▭	County border

SEE ALSO

- *Where to Stay* pp128–33

- *Where to Eat* pp138–45

GETTING AROUND

Several motorways and main roads fan out from Dublin. The M1 goes north to Dundalk, the N11 south, following the scenic coastline. Regular train services operate around the country from Heuston and Connolly stations. Coach services also run all around the country from Dublin. The DART railway line runs north and south from the city along the coast and has several stops in central Dublin.

Castletown House ❶

See pp106–7.

Robertstown ❷

Co Kildare. 🚶 *240.* 🚌

Ten locks west along the Grand Canal from Dublin, Robertstown is a characteristic 19th-century canalside village, with warehouses and cottages flanking the waterfront. Freight barges plied the route until about 1960, but pleasure boats have since replaced them. Visitors can take barge cruises from the quay and the Grand Canal Company's Hotel, built in 1801 for canal passengers, is now used for banquets.

Near Sallins, about 8 km (5 miles) east of Robertstown, the canal is carried over the River Liffey along the **Leinster Aqueduct**, an impressive structure built in 1783.

Bog of Allen Nature Centre ❸

Lullymore, Co Kildare. **Tel** *045 860133.* 🚌 *to Newbridge & Kildare.* 🚌 *to Allenwood.* ⬜ *all year: 10am–4pm Mon–Fri.* 📷 ♿ *limited.* **www**.*ipcc.ie*

Anyone interested in the natural history of Irish bogs should visit the Nature Centre, an exhibition housed in an old farm at Lullymore, 9 km (6 miles) northeast of Rathangan. It lies at the heart of the Bog of Allen, a vast expanse of raised bog that extends across the counties of Offaly, Laois and Kildare.

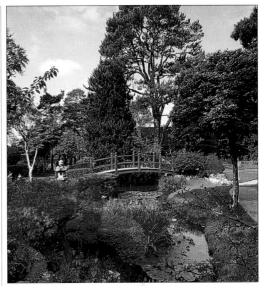
Japanese Gardens at Tully near Kildare

The exhibition explains the history and ecology of the bog, and features displays of flora and fauna as well as archaeological finds from the surrounding area. Guided walks are also organized to introduce visitors to the bog's delicate ecosystem and the careful conservation work that is being done.

Stacking peat for use as fuel

Monasterevin ❹

Co Kildare. 🚶 *2,200.* 🚌

This Georgian market town lies west of Kildare, where the Grand Canal crosses the River Barrow. Waterborne trade brought prosperity to Monasterevin in the 18th century, but the locks now see little traffic. However, you can still admire the aqueduct, which is a superb example of canal engineering. **Moore Abbey**, next to the church, was built in the 18th century on the site of a Cistercian monastery which was founded by St Evin, but the grand Gothic mansion owes a great deal to Victorian remodelling. Originally the ancestral seat of the earls of Drogheda, in the 1920s Moore Abbey became the home of the internationally celebrated Irish tenor, John McCormack. It has now been turned into a hospital.

Kildare ❺

Co Kildare. 🚶 *4,200.* 🚌 🚌 📷 *Market House, May–Sep: 045 521 240.* 🛍 *Thu.*

The charming and tidy town of Kildare is dominated by **St Brigid's Cathedral**, which commemorates the saint who founded a religious community on this site in AD 480. Unusually, monks and nuns lived

The Grand Canal Company's Hotel in Robertstown

here under the same roof, but this was not the only unorthodox practice associated with the community. Curious pagan rituals, including the burning of a perpetual fire, continued until the 16th century. The fire pit is visible in the grounds today. So too is a round tower, which was probably built in the 12th century and has a Romanesque doorway. The cathedral was rebuilt in the Victorian era, but the restorers largely adhered to the original 13th-century design.

St Brigid's Cathedral
Market Square. ☐ May–Sep: daily. 🖼 donation. ♿

Environs
Kildare lies at the heart of racing country: the Curragh racecourse is nearby, stables are scattered all around and bloodstock sales take place at Kill, northeast of town.

The **National Stud** is a semi state-run bloodstock farm at Tully, just south of Kildare. It was founded in 1900 by an eccentric Anglo-Irish colonel, William Hall-Walker. He sold his foals on the basis of their astrological charts, and put skylights in the stables to allow the horses to be "touched" by sunlight or moonbeams. Hall-Walker received the title Lord Wavertree in reward for bequeathing the farm to the British Crown in 1915.

Visitors can explore the 400-ha (1,000-acre) grounds and watch the horses being exercised. Mares and stallions are kept in separate paddocks. The breeding stallions are expected to cover more than 100

HORSE RACING IN IRELAND
Ireland has a strong racing culture and, thanks to its non-elitist image, the sport is enjoyed by all. Much of the thoroughbred industry centres around the Curragh, a grassy plain in County Kildare stretching unfenced for more than 2,000 ha (5,000 acres). This area is home to many of the country's studs and training yards, and every morning horses are put through their paces on the gallops. Most of the major flat races, including the Irish Derby, take place at the Curragh racecourse just east of Kildare. Other popular fixtures are held at nearby Punchestown – most famously the steeplechase festival in April – and at Leopardstown, which also hosts major National Hunt races *(see p29)*.

Finishing straight at the Curragh racecourse

mares per season. There is a foaling unit where the mare and foal can rest for a few days after the birth.

The farm has its own forge and saddlery, and also a Horse Museum. Housed in old stable block, this illustrates the importance of horses in Irish life. Exhibits include the frail skeleton of Arkle, the champion steeplechaser who raced to fame in the 1960s.

Sharing the same estate as the National Stud are the **Japanese Gardens**, created by Lord Wavertree at the height of the Edwardian penchant for Orientalism. The gardens were laid out in 1906–10 by a Japanese landscape gardener called Tassa Eida, with the help of his son Minoru and 40 assistants. The impres-

sive array of trees and shrubs includes maples, mulberries, bonsai, magnolias, cherry trees and sacred bamboos.

The gardens take the form of an allegorical journey from the cradle to the grave, beginning with life emerging from the Gate of Oblivion (a cave) and leading to the Gateway of Eternity, a Zen rock garden.

St Fiachra's Garden was a millennium project completed in 1999. It was designed by Professor Martin Hallinan and commemorates St Fiachra, the Patron Saint of Gardeners.

🍁 National Stud, Japanese & St Fiachra Gardens
Tully. **Tel** 045 521617. ☐ mid-Feb–mid-Nov: 9:30am–5pm daily. 🖼 ♿ 🅿 Stud only. 🅿 📷 **www**.irish-national-stud.ie

St Brigid's Cathedral and roofless round tower in Kildare town

Castletown House ●

Built in 1722–32 for William Conolly, the Speaker of the Irish Parliament, the façade of Castletown was the work of Florentine architect Alessandro Galilei and gave Ireland its first taste of Palladianism. The magnificent interiors date from the second half of the 18th century. They were commissioned by Lady Louisa Lennox, wife of William Conolly's great-nephew, Tom, who lived here from 1759. Castletown remained in the family until 1965, when it was taken over by the Irish Georgian Society. The state now owns the house and it is open to the public.

Conolly crest on an armchair

★ Long Gallery
The heavy ceiling sections and friezes date from the 1720s and the walls were decorated in the Pompeian manner in the 1770s.

Green drawing room

Red drawing room
The red damask covering the walls of this room is probably French and dates from the 19th century. This exquisite mahogany bureau was made for Lady Louisa in the 1760s.

West wing with kitchen

The Dining Room with the compartmentalized ceiling was designed by Isaac Ware.

Boudoir wall paintings
The boudoir's decorative panels, moved here from the Long Gallery, were inspired by the Raphael Loggia in the Vatican.

VISITORS' CHECKLIST

Celbridge, Co Kildare.
Tel 628 8252. 🚌 67, 67A
from Dublin. 🕐 Easter Day–
Sep: 10am–6pm Mon–Fri,
1–6pm Sat, Sun, public hols;
Oct: 10am–5pm Mon–Fri,
1–5pm Sun, public hols.
📷 ♿ 🚻 🛍 obligatory.
Summer concerts.

★ Print room

In this, the only intact 18th-century print room in Ireland, Lady Louisa indulged her taste for Italian engravings. It was fashionable at the time for ladies to paste prints directly on to the wall and frame them with elaborate festoons.

The Boar Hunt, painted by
Paul de Vos (1596–1678)

★ Staircase hall
This portrait of Lady Louisa is part of the superb Rococo stuccowork by the Francini brothers which decorates the staircase.

The east wing originally
housed the stables.

Entrance

The entrance hall is an
austere Neo-Classical room.
Its most decorative feature is
the delicate carving on the
pilasters of the upper gallery.

STAR FEATURES

★ Long Gallery

★ Print room

★ Staircase hall

CONOLLY'S FOLLY

This folly, which lies just
beyond the grounds of
Castletown House, provides
the focus of the view from
the Long Gallery. Speaker
Conolly's widow, Katherine,
commissioned it in 1740
as a memorial to her late
husband, and to provide
employment after a harsh
winter. The unusual structure
of superimposed arches
crowned by an obelisk was
designed by Richard Castle,
architect of Russborough
House *(see p108)*.

Saloon in Russborough House with original fireplace and stuccowork

Russborough House ❻

Blessington, Co Wicklow. **Tel** 045 865239. 🚌 65 from Dublin (check times). ⏰ May–Sep: 10am–5pm daily; Apr & Oct: 10am–5pm Sun & public hols only. 🎫 📷 obligatory.
🛈 📷

This Palladian mansion, built in the 1740s for Joseph Leeson, later Earl of Milltown, is one of Ireland's finest houses. Its architect, a German called Richard Castle, also designed Powerscourt House (see pp114–15) and is credited with introducing the Palladian style to Ireland. Unlike many grand estates in the Pale, Russborough has survived magnificently, both inside and out. The house claims the longest frontage in Ireland, with a façade adorned by heraldic lions and curved colonnades. The interior is even more impressive. Many rooms feature superb stucco decoration, which was done largely by the Italian Francini brothers, who also worked on Castletown House

Vernet seascape in the drawing room

(see pp106–7). The best examples are found in the music room, saloon and library, which are embellished with exuberant foliage and cherubs. Around the main staircase, a riot of Rococo plasterwork depicts a hunt, with hounds clasping garlands of flowers. The stucco mouldings in the drawing room were designed especially to enclose marine scenes by the French artist, Joseph Vernet (1714–89). The paintings were sold in 1926, but were tracked down more than 40 years afterwards and returned to the house.

Russborough House has many other treasures to be seen, including finely worked fireplaces made of Italian marble, imposing mahogany doorways and priceless collections of silver, porcelain and Gobelins tapestries.

Such riches aside, one of the principal reasons to visit Russborough is to see the **Beit Art Collection**, famous for its Flemish, Dutch and Spanish Old Master paintings. Sir Alfred Beit, who bought the house in 1952, inherited the pictures from his uncle – also named Alfred Beit. The family's wealth had come from gold mines and

---

THE HISTORY OF THE PALE

The term "Pale" refers to an area around Dublin which marked the limits of English influence from Norman to Tudor times. The frontier fluctuated but, at its largest, the Pale stretched from Dundalk in County Louth to Waterford town. Gaelic chieftains outside the area could keep their lands provided they agreed to raise their heirs within the Pale.

The Palesmen supported their rulers' interests and considered themselves the upholders of English values. This widened the gap between the Gaelic majority and the Anglo-Irish, foretelling England's doomed involvement in the country. Long after its fortifications were dismantled, the idea of the Pale lived on as a state of mind. The expression "beyond the pale" survives as a definition of those outside the bounds of civilized society.

An 18th-century family enjoying the privileged lifestyle that was typical within the Pale

diamond dealing in Kimberley, South Africa. The Beit family donated Russborough to the Beit Foundation, opening the house to the public while living in one of the wings of the house.

In 1974, 1986, 2000 and 2001, several masterpieces were stolen from the house, but all were later retrieved. Only a selection of paintings is on view at any one time, while others are on permanent loan to the National Gallery in the centre of Dublin (*see pp48–51*). Other paintings from the National Gallery are also on view in the house from time to time.

Russborough enjoys a fine position near the village of **Blessington**, which has a good view of the Wicklow Mountains. The house lies in the midst of wooded parkland rather than elaborate gardens. As Alfred Beit said of Irish Palladianism, "Fine architecture standing in a green sward was considered enough".

Environs
The **Poulaphouca Reservoir**, formed by the damming of the River Liffey, extends south from Blessington. The placid lake is popular with water-sports enthusiasts, especially in summer, while others come simply to enjoy the lovely views of the nearby Wicklow Mountains.

Avondale House, with its colourful gardens in the foreground

Browne's Hill Dolmen ❼

Co Carlow. 🚌 🚆 to Carlow. 🅿 daily.

In a field 3 km (2 miles) east of Carlow, along the R726, stands a huge dolmen boasting the biggest capstone in Ireland. It stands in the area of Browne's Hill, where there is a stone house dating from 1763. Weighing a reputed 100 tonnes, this massive stone is embedded in the earth at one end and supported at the other by three much smaller stones. Dating back to 2000 BC, the Dolmen is thought to mark the tomb of a local chieftain. A path from the road skirts the field before reaching it.

Avondale House ❽

Co Wicklow. **Tel** *0404 46111.* 🚌 🚆 to Rathdrum. **House and grounds** 🅿 mid-Mar–Oct: 11am–6pm daily (last adm to house: 5pm). 🅿 Mar–Apr, Sep–Oct: Mon, Good Fri. 🏵 🍴 🛈

Lying just south of Rathdrum, Avondale House was the birthplace of the 19th-century politician and patriot, Charles Stewart Parnell (*see p17*). Built in 1779, it passed into the hands of the Parnell family in 1795 and Charles Stewart was born here on 27 June 1846. The Georgian mansion now houses a museum dedicated to Parnell and the fight for Home Rule. The birthplace of Irish Forestry, Avondale is managed by the Irish Forestry Board but the public is free to explore the 200 ha (512 acres) of grounds, complete with picnic and children's play areas. Known as **Avondale Forest Park**, the former estate includes an impressive arboretum which was first planted in the 18th century and has had many additions made to it since 1900.

There are some lovely walks through the woods, including the magnificent Great Ride, which is one of the best, with pleasant views along the River Avonmore. There is also much wildlife in the area, including hares, rabbits and otters.

Parnell's chair in Avondale House

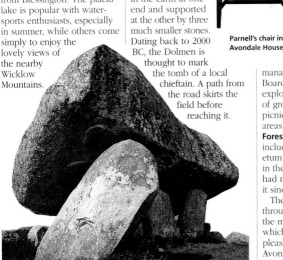

Browne's Hill Dolmen, famous for its enormous capstone

Glendalough 9

Co Wicklow. *St Kevin's bus from Dublin.* **Ruins** ○ *daily.* ✔ *in summer.* **Visitors' centre** *Tel 0404 45325/45352.* ○ *9:30am–5:15pm daily.* ● *24–27 Dec.* ♿ 🎥 ✔ *on request.* **www**.*heritageireland.ie*

The steep, wooded slopes of Glendalough, the "valley of the two lakes", harbour one of Ireland's most atmospheric monastic sites. Established by St Kevin in the 6th century, the settlement was sacked time and again by the Vikings but nevertheless flourished for over 600 years. Decline set in only after English forces partially razed the site in 1398, though it functioned as a monastic centre until the Dissolution of the Monasteries in 1539 *(see p14)*. Pilgrims kept on coming to Glendalough even after that, particularly on St Kevin's feast day, 3 June, which was often a riotous event.

The age of the buildings is uncertain, but most date from the 8th to 12th centuries. Many

View along the Upper Lake at Glendalough

were restored in the 1870s. The main group of ruins lies east of the Lower Lake, but other buildings associated with St Kevin are found by the Upper Lake. Here, where the scenery is much wilder, it is possible to enjoy more the tranquillity of Glendalough and to escape the crowds which inevitably descend on the site. Try to arrive as early as possible in the day, particularly during the peak tourist season. Enter the monastery through the double stone arch of the **Gatehouse**, the only surviving example in Ireland of a gateway into a monastic enclosure.

A short walk leads to a graveyard with a **Round tower** in one corner. Reaching 30 m (100 ft) in height, this is one of the finest of its kind in the country. Its cap was rebuilt in the 1870s using stones found inside the tower. The roofless **Cathedral** nearby dates mainly

Remains of the Gatehouse, the original entrance to Glendalough

St Kevin's Kitchen

from the 12th century and is the valley's largest ruin. At the centre of the churchyard stands the tiny **Priests' House**, whose name derives from the fact that it was a burial place for local clergy. The worn carving of a robed figure above the door is thought possibly to be St Kevin, flanked by two disciples. East of here, **St Kevin's Cross** dates from the 8th century and is one of the best preserved of Glendalough's various High Crosses. Made of granite, the cross may once have marked the boundary of the monastic cemetery. Below, nestled in the lush valley, a tiny oratory with a steeply pitched stone roof is a charming sight. Erected in the 11th century or even earlier, it is popularly known as **St Kevin's Kitchen**; this is perhaps because its belfry, which is thought to be a later addition, resembles a chimney. One of the earliest churches at Glendalough, **St**

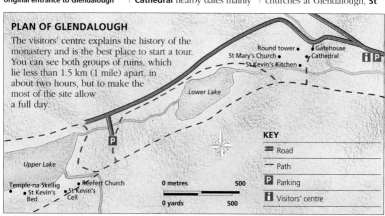

PLAN OF GLENDALOUGH

The visitors' centre explains the history of the monastery and is the best place to start a tour. You can see both groups of ruins, which lie less than 1.5 km (1 mile) apart, in about two hours, but to make the most of the site allow a full day.

Round tower ● ◆ Gatehouse
St Mary's Church ●   ● Cathedral
── St Kevin's Kitchen ●

Lower Lake

Upper Lake

Temple-na-Skellig ●   ● Reefert Church
● St Kevin's ● St Kevin's
  Bed   Cell

0 metres   500
0 yards   500

KEY

▦ Road

-- Path

🅿 Parking

🛈 Visitors' centre

ST KEVIN AT GLENDALOUGH

St Kevin was born in 498, a descendant of the royal house of Leinster. He rejected his life of privilege, however, choosing to live instead as a hermit in a cave at Glendalough. He later founded a monastery here, and went on to establish a notable centre of learning devoted to the care of the sick and the copying and illumination of manuscripts. St Kevin attracted many disciples to Glendalough during his lifetime, but the monastery became more celebrated as a place of pilgrimage after his death in around 618.

Colourful legends about the saint make up for the dearth of facts about him. That he lived to the age of 120 is just one of the many stories told about him. Another tale claims that one day, when St Kevin was at prayer, a blackbird laid an egg in one of his outstretched hands. According to legend the saint remained in the same position until the bird was hatched.

have been used as a tomb in the Bronze Age, but it is more famous as St Kevin's favourite retreat. It was from this point that the saint allegedly rejected the advances of a naked woman by picking her up and throwing her into the lake.

Mount Usher Gardens ⑩

Ashford, Co Wicklow. **Tel** 0404 40116. ⬛ to Ashford. ⬤ 21 Apr–31 Oct: 10:30am–6pm daily (last adm: 5:20pm). ▨ ⬛ ⬜ (27 Apr–31 Oct). ♿ limited. 🎫 call to book. **www**.mount-usher-gardens.com

Set on the banks of the River Vartry, just east of Ashford, are the Mount Usher Gardens. They were designed in 1868 by a Dubliner, Edward Walpole, who imbued them with his strong sense of romanticism.

The 8 ha (20 acres) are laid out in a wild, informal style and contain around 4,000 different species of plants including rare shrubs and trees, from Chinese conifers and bamboos to Mexican pines and pampas grass. The Maple Walk is particularly glorious in the autumn, and in spring the rhododendron collection is brilliant with reds and pinks.

The river provides the main focus of the Mount Usher Gardens and, amid the exotic and lush vegetation, the visitor can usually catch a glimpse of herons standing on the many weirs and little bridges that cross the river.

Round tower at Glendalough

Mary's, lies across a field to the west. Some traces of hood moulding (intended to throw off water) are visible outside the east window. The path along the south bank of the river leads visitors to the Upper Lake. This is the site of more monastic ruins and is also the chief starting point for walks through the valley and to a number of abandoned lead and zinc mines.

Situated in a grove not far from the Poulanass waterfall are the ruins of the **Reefert Church**, a simple building. Its unusual name is a corruption of *Righ Fearta*, meaning "burial place of the kings"; the church may mark the site of an

ancient cemetery. Nearby, on a rocky spur overlooking the Upper Lake, stands **St Kevin's Cell**, the foundation of a beehive-shaped structure which is thought to have once been the home of the hermit.

There are two sites on the south side of the lake which cannot be reached on foot but are visible from the shore on the other side. **Temple-na-Skellig**, or the "church on the rock", was supposedly built on the site of the first church that was founded by St Kevin at Glendalough. To the east of it, carved into the cliff, is **St Kevin's Bed**. This small cave, in fact little more than a rocky ledge, is thought possibly to

Mount Usher Gardens, on the banks of the River Vartry

A Tour of the Military Road ⑪

Rare red squirrel

The British built the Military Road through the heart of the Wicklow Mountains during a campaign to flush out Irish rebels after an uprising in 1798 *(see p16)*. Now known as the R115, this winding road takes you through the emptiest and most rugged landscapes of County Wicklow. Beautiful countryside, in which deer and other wildlife flourish, is characteristic of the whole of this tour.

Glencree ①
The former British barracks in Glencree are among several found along the Military Road.

Powerscourt Waterfall ⑨
The River Dargle cascades 130 m (425 ft) over a granite escarpment to form Ireland's highest waterfall.

Great Sugar Loaf ⑧
The granite cone of Great Sugar Loaf Mountain can be climbed in under an hour from the car park on its southern side.

Sally Gap ②
This remote pass is surrounded by a vast expanse of blanket bog dotted with pools and streams.

Glenmacnass ③
After Sally Gap, the road drops into a deep glen where a waterfall spills dramatically over rocks.

Lough Tay ⑦
Stark, rocky slopes plunge down to the dark waters of Lough Tay. Though it lies within a Guinness-owned estate, the lake is accessible to walkers.

Roundwood ⑥
The highest village in Ireland at 238 m (780 ft) above sea level, Roundwood enjoys a fine setting. Its main street is lined with pubs, cafés and craft shops.

Glendalough ④
This ancient monastery *(see pp110–11)*, enclosed by wooded slopes, is the prime historical sight in the Wicklow Mountains.

TIPS FOR DRIVERS

Length: 96 km (60 miles).
Stopping-off points: There are several pubs and cafés in Enniskerry (including Poppies, an old-fashioned tearoom), and also in Roundwood, but this area is better suited for picnics. There are numerous marked picnic spots south of Enniskerry.

0 kilometres 5

0 miles 3

KEY

▬▬▬ Tour route

═══ Other roads

☼ Viewpoint

Vale of Clara ⑤
This picturesque wooded valley follows the River Avonmore. It contains the tiny village of Clara, which consists of two houses, a church and a school.

Wicklow Mountains ⑫

Co Wicklow. 🚌 to Rathdrum & Wicklow. 🚌 to Enniskerry, Wicklow, Glendalough, Rathdrum & Avoca. 🏛 Rialto House, Fitzwilliam Square, Wicklow, 0404 69117. www.eastcoastmidlands.ie

The inaccessibility of the rugged Wicklow Mountains meant that they once provided a safe hideout for opponents of English rule. Rebels who took part in the 1798 uprising sought refuge here. The building of the **Military Road**, started in 1800, made the area slightly more accessible, but the mountains are still thinly populated. There is little traffic to disturb enjoyment of the exhilarating scenery of rock-strewn glens, lush forest and bogland where heather gives a purple sheen to the land. Turf-cutting is still a thriving cottage industry, and you can often see peat stacked up by the road. Numerous walking trails weave through these landscapes. Among them is the **Wicklow Way**, which extends 132 km (82 miles) from Marlay Park in Dublin to Clonegal in County Carlow. It is marked but not always easy to follow, so do not set out without a good map. Although no peak exceeds 915 m (3,000 ft), the Wicklow Mountains can be dangerous in bad weather.

A good starting point for exploring the northern area is the picture-postcard estate village of **Enniskerry**, close to

View across the Long Ponds to Killruddery House

Powerscourt *(see pp114–15)*. To the south, you can reach Glendalough *(see pp110–11)* and the **Vale of Avoca**. The beauty of this gentle valley was captured in the poetry of Thomas Moore (1779–1852): "There is not in the wide world a valley so sweet as that vale in whose bosom the bright waters meet" – a reference to the confluence of the Avonbeg and Avonmore rivers, the so-called **Meeting of the Waters** beyond Avondale House *(see p109)*. Nestled among wooded hills at the heart of the valley is the hamlet of Avoca, where the **Avoca Handweavers** produce colourful tweeds in the oldest hand-weaving mill in Ireland, in operation since 1723.

Further north, towards the coast near Ashford, the River Vartry rushes through the deep chasm of the **Devil's Glen**. On entering the valley, the river falls 30 m (100 ft) into a pool known as the Devil's

Punchbowl. There are good walks around here, with fine views of the coast.

🏛 Avoca Handweavers
Avoca. **Tel** 0402 35105.
◯ 9:30am–5:30pm daily.
● 25/26 Dec. **Weaving shed**
◯ 8am–4:30pm Mon–Fri,
10am–5pm Sat & Sun. 🍴 🏛 ♿

Killruddery House and Gardens ⑬

Bray, Co Wicklow. **Tel** 0404 46024.
Gardens ◯ Apr: 1–5pm Sat, Sun;
May–Sep: 1–5pm daily. **House**
◯ May, Jun, Sep: 1–5pm daily. 🎧
♿ limited. www.killruddery.com

Killruddery House lies just to the south of Bray, in the shadow of Little Sugar Loaf Mountain. Built in 1651, it has been the seat of the Earls of Meath ever since, although it was remodelled in the 1800s.

The house contains some good carving and stuccowork. The real charm stems from its formal gardens. Laid out in the 1680s by a French gardener named Bonet, who also worked at Versailles, they feature romantic parterres and an array of hedges, trees and shrubs. The sylvan theatre, a small enclosure surrounded by a bay hedge, is the only known example in Ireland.

The garden centres on the Long Ponds, a pair of canals which extend 165 m (550 ft) and were once used to stock fish. Beyond, an enclosed pool leads to a Victorian arrangement of paths flanked by statues and hedges of yew, beech, lime and hornbeam.

Colourful moorland around Sally Gap in the Wicklow Mountains

Powerscourt ⑭

Laocöon statue on upper terrace

The gardens at Powerscourt are probably the finest in Ireland, both for their design and their dramatic setting at the foot of Great Sugar Loaf Mountain. The house and grounds were commissioned in the 1730s by Richard Wingfield, the first Viscount Powerscourt. The gardens fell into decline but, in 1840, the original scheme was revived. New ornamental gardens were completed in 1858–75 by the seventh Viscount, who added gates, urns and statues collected during his travels on the Continent. Gutted by an accidental fire in 1974, the ground floor and the ballroom on the first floor have been renovated.

Bamberg Gate
Made in Vienna in the 1770s, this gilded wrought-iron gate was brought to Powerscourt by the seventh Viscount from Bamberg Cathedral in Bavaria.

The walled gardens include a formal arrangement of clipped laurel trees but are also used for growing plants for Powerscourt's gardens.

Entrance

Statue of Laocöon

The pets' cemetery contains the graves of Wingfield family dogs, cats and even horses and cattle.

Dolphin pond
This pool, designed as a fish pond in the 18th century, is enclosed by exotic conifers in a lovely secluded garden.

POWERSCOURT HOUSE

In 1974 a fire at the Palladian mansion at Powerscourt left the building a burnt-out shell. The Slazenger family, who now own the estate, have restored part of the house; the ground floor now incorporates a terrace café, speciality shops and house exhibition describing the history of the estate. Originally built in 1731 on the site of a Norman castle, the house was designed by Richard Castle, also the architect of Russborough House (see p108).

Powerscourt ablaze in 1974

★ The Perron

This superb Italianate stairway, added in 1874, leads down to the Triton Lake, which is guarded by two statues of the winged horse Pegasus and the emblem of the Wingfield family.

VISITORS' CHECKLIST

Enniskerry, Co Wicklow. **Tel** 204 6000. Alpine Coach from Bray DART station. 9:30am–5:30pm daily (gardens open until dusk in winter). 25 & 26 Dec. www.powerscourt.ie

The Italian garden is laid out on terraces which were first cut into the steep hillside in the 1730s.

Pebble mosaic

Many tonnes of pebbles were gathered from nearby Bray beach to build the Perron and to make this mosaic on the terrace.

The Pepper Pot Tower was built in 1911.

★ Triton Lake

Made for the first garden, the lake takes its name from its central fountain, which is modelled on a 17th-century work by Bernini in Rome.

★ Japanese gardens

These enchanting Edwardian gardens, created out of bogland, contain Chinese conifers and bamboo trees.

STAR FEATURES

★ The Perron

★ Japanese gardens

★ Triton Lake

Bray ⑮

Co Wicklow. 🚶 33,000. 🚉 DART.
🅿️ ℹ️ Old Court House, Main St,
286 7128/286 6796. www.bray.ie

Once a refined Victorian
resort, Bray is nowadays a
brash holiday town, with
amusement arcades and fish-
and-chip shops lining the
seafront. Its beach attracts huge
crowds in summer, including
many young families. Anyone
in search of peace and quiet
can escape to nearby Bray
Head, where there is scope for
bracing cliffside walks. Bray
also makes a good base from
which to explore the Wicklow
Mountains *(see p113)*, the
delightful coastal villages of
Killiney and Dalkey *(see p91)*
and Powerscourt House and
Gardens *(see pp114–15).*

**Tourist road train on the seafront
esplanade at Bray**

Newbridge Demesne ⑯

Donabate, Co Dublin. **Tel** 843 6534.
🚉 to Donabate. 🚌 33B from
Swords. **House and Courtyard** ◯
Apr–Sep: 10am–5pm Tue–Sat, noon–
6pm Sun & public hols; Oct–Mar:
noon–5pm Sat, Sun & public hols.
⬤ 25–26 Dec. 📷 🎫 house only
(obligatory). ♿ courtyard only. **Park**
◯ daily. www.fingal-dublin.com

Newbridge is located on the
edge of the seaside village of
Donabate, 19 km (12 miles)
north of Dublin. The house
itself is a delight for enthusiasts
of Georgian architecture and
decor. The house was designed
by George Semple in 1737 for
Archbishop Charles Cobbe,
and it remained the family

Connemara Pony stabled at Newbridge House

home until 1986, when it was
bought by the local council.
The Cobbe family retains the
use of the upstairs quarters.

The highlight of the house
tour is the red drawing room,
one of the best-preserved
Georgian rooms in the country.
Its rich red decor is complemented by fine plasterwork
by Richard Williams and by
some impressive portrait and
landscape paintings. Its contents have remained unaltered
since at least the 1820s.

Also on view are the sizeable, airy dining room, a large
kitchen with a huge stock of
utensils, and the Museum of
Curiosities – a small room
filled to the rafters with
artifacts collected from 1790
onwards by Cobbe family
members on their foreign
travels. Housed in cabinets,
some of which date back to
the late 1700s, are unusual
and bizarre items such as
delicately carved ostrich eggs,
snakeskins and stuffed animals.

The cobbled courtyard has
been restored and now has
displays of aspects of late
18th-century life, including

dairy production,
carpentry and
forging. This
and the new
playground
make it a
popular spot
with families.
It also houses
rare goat and
pony breeds,
including the
native Conne-
mara pony, as
well as a pleasant tea room.
The Lord Chancellor's intricately detailed ceremonial
carriage which is on loan
from the National Museum
(see pp44–5) is an incongruous
exhibit but considered to be
one of the best examples of
carriagework in existence.

Footpaths wind through the
woodland, and the elegant,
rolling grounds of Newbridge,
which are attractively landscaped in the style of an
English estate.

Ardgillan Demesne ⑰

Balbriggan, Co Dublin. **Tel** 849 2212.
🚌 33 via Skerries to Balbriggan.
Castle ◯ Apr–Sep: 11am–6pm Tue–
Sun & public hols (Jul–Aug: daily);
Oct–Mar: 11am–4:30pm Tue–Sun &
public hols. ⬤ 23 Dec–1 Jan. 📷 ♿
except kitchen. **Park and Gardens**
◯ daily. www.visitdublin.com

In between the very likeable
resort towns of Skerries
and Balbriggan, the Ardgillan
Demesne is set on a high
stretch of coastline and offers

The elegant façade of Newbridge House

Stately drawing room in Ardgillan Castle

a particularly pleasant vantage point for stunning views over Drogheda Bay. Its sweeping and expansive grounds, which cover 78 ha (194 acres), incorporate various ornamental gardens, including a rose garden and a walled kitchen garden, as well as rolling pasture and dense woodland (the name Ardgillan means "high wooded area").

In the grounds stands Ardgillan Castle, which was built in 1737 by the Reverend Robert Taylor. The rooms on the ground floor are all furnished in Georgian and Victorian styles and the basement kitchen also retains its original decor. Upstairs there is an exhibition space which houses a permanent collection of old maps.

Gramophone in the Millmount Museum

Drogheda ⑱

Co Louth. 🏘 28,000. 🚆 🚌
ℹ️ Bus Station, Donore Rd, 041 9837070, 9am–5pm Mon–Fri, 9am–4:30pm Sat. 📅 Sat.

In the 14th century, this historic Norman port near the mouth of the River Boyne was one of Ireland's most important towns. It was first captured by the Danes in AD 911 and later heavily fortified by the Normans. However, the place seems never to have fully recovered from a vicious attack by the English general Oliver Cromwell in 1649, during which 3,000 citizens were killed after refusing to surrender. Although it looks rather dilapidated today, the town has retained its original street plan and has a rich medieval heritage. Little is left of Drogheda's Norman defences but **St Lawrence Gate**, a fine 13th-century barbican, has survived. The **Butter Gate** is the only other surviving gate. Near St Lawrence Gate there are two churches called **St Peter's**. The one belonging to the Church of Ireland, built in 1753, is the more striking and has some splendid gravestones. The Catholic church, on West Street and dating from 1791, is worth visiting just to see the embalmed head of Oliver Plunkett, an archbishop who was martyred in 1681. It is displayed in an elaborate glass case beside its certificate of authenticity, dated 1682.

South of the river you can climb Millmount, a Norman motte that is topped by a Martello tower. As well as providing a good view, this is the site of the **Millmount Museum**, which contains an interesting display of artifacts relating to the town and its history, as well as a number of craft workshops.

🏛 **Millmount Museum**
Millmount Square. **Tel** 041 983 3097.
📅 daily. 🔴 10 days at Christmas.
📷 🅿️ ♿ www.millmount.net

Monasterboice ⑲

Co Louth. 🚆 to Drogheda. 📅 daily.

Founded in the 5th century by an obscure disciple of St Patrick called St Buite, this monastic settlement is one of the most famous religious sites in Ireland. The ruins of the medieval monastery are enclosed within a graveyard in a lovely secluded spot to the north of Drogheda. The site includes a roofless round tower and two churches, but Monasterboice's greatest treasures are its 10th-century High Crosses, carved to help educate an illiterate populace.

Muiredach's High Cross is the finest of its kind in Ireland, and its sculpted biblical scenes are still remarkably fresh. They depict the life of Christ on the west face, while the east face features mainly Old Testament scenes. These include Moses striking the rock to get water for the Israelites and David struggling with Goliath. The cross is named after an inscription on the base which reads: "A prayer for Muiredach by whom this cross was made", which, it is thought, may refer to the abbot of Monasterboice.

The 6.5-m (21-ft) West Cross, also known as the Tall Cross, is one of the largest in Ireland. The carving has not lasted as well as on Muiredach's Cross, but scenes from the Death of Christ can still be made out. The North Cross, which is the least notable of the three, features a Crucifixion illustration and a carved spiral pattern.

Round tower and West High Cross at Monasterboice

Thatched cottage in Carlingford on the mountainous Cooley Peninsula

Carlingford ⑳

Co Louth. 👥 650. 🚌
ℹ️ **Holy Trinity Heritage Centre**
Churchyard Rd, 042 9373454. ⬜
10am–12:30pm, 2–4:30pm Mon–Fri.
www.fjordlands.org **Carlingford**
Adventure Centre *Tholsel St.* **Tel**
042 9373100. ⬜ *9am–5:30pm*
daily. ⬛ *two weeks at Christmas.*
www.carlingfordadventure.com

This is a picturesque fishing
village, located between the
mountains of the Cooley
Peninsula and the waters of
Carlingford Lough. The border
with Northern Ireland runs
right through the centre of this
drowned river valley, and from
the village you can look across
to the Mountains of Mourne
on the Ulster side. Carlingford
is an interesting place, with its
pretty whitewashed cottages
and ancient buildings clustered
along medieval alleyways.
The ruins of **King John's
Castle**, built by the Normans
to protect the entrance to the
lough, still dominate the
village. The **Holy Trinity
Heritage Centre**, which is
housed in a medieval church,
tells the history of the port
from Anglo-Norman times.
    Carlingford is the country's
oyster capital, and its oyster
festival in August draws large
crowds. The lough is popular
for watersports and in summer
cruises leave from the quay.
    Carlingford is well placed for
hikes on the Cooley Peninsula.
The **Carlingford Adventure
Centre** provides information
on walking and water activities.

Environs
A scenic route weaves around
the **Cooley Peninsula**, skirting
the coast and then cutting

through the mountains. The
section along the north coast
is the most dramatic: just
3 km (2 miles) northwest
of Carlingford, in the
**Slieve Foye Forest
Park**, a road climbs to
give a breathtaking
view over the hills
and lough.
    The Táin Trail,
which you can join
at Carlingford, is a 30-
km (19-mile) circuit
through some of the
peninsula's most rug-
ged scenery, with cairns and
other prehistoric sites dotted
over the moorland. Keen
hikers can walk it in a day.

Dundalk ㉑

Co Louth. 👥 30,000. 🚆 🚌 ℹ️
Jocelyn St, 042 9335484. 🛒 *Thu.*

Dundalk once marked the
northernmost point of the
Pale, the area controlled by
the English during the Middle
Ages (*see p108*). Now, lying
midway between Dublin and
Belfast, it is the last major
town before you reach the
Northern Ireland border.
    Dundalk is the gateway to
the Cooley Peninsula, but
there is little worth stopping
for in the town itself.
However, the **County
Museum**, which is housed
in an 18th-century distillery,
gives an insight into some of
Louth's traditional industries,
such as beer-making.

🏛️ **County Museum**
Jocelyn St. **Tel** *042 9327056.*
⬜ *May–Oct: 10:30am–5:30pm
Mon–Sat, 2–6pm Sun.* ⬛ *24 Dec–
2 Jan.* 🚫 ♿ **www**.louthcoco.ie

Mellifont Abbey ㉒

Cullen, Co Louth. **Tel** *041 9826459.*
🚆 *to Drogheda.* 🚌 *to Drogheda
or Slane.* ⬜ *May–Oct: 10am–6pm
daily (last adm: 5:15pm).* 🚫
www.heritageireland.ie

On the banks of the River
Mattock, 10 km (6 miles) west
of Drogheda, lies the first
Cistercian monastery built in
Ireland. Mellifont was founded
in 1142 on the orders of St
Malachy, the Archbishop of
Armagh. He was influenced by
St Bernard, who was behind
the success of the Cistercian
Order in Europe. St Malachy
introduced not only Cistercian
rigour to Mellifont, but also
the formal style of
monastic architecture
used on the conti-
nent. In 1539, the
abbey was closed
and turned into a for-
tified house. William
of Orange used it as
his headquarters
during the Battle of
the Boyne in 1690.
It is now a ruin, but it is still
possible to appreciate the
scale and plan of the original
complex. Little survives of the
abbey church but, to the south
of it, enclosed by what is left
of the Roman-
esque cloister,
is the most
interesting
building at
Mellifont: a
13th-century
lavabo where
monks came
to wash

**Glazed medieval tiles
at Mellifont Abbey**

Ruined lavabo at Mellifont Abbey

THE BATTLE OF THE BOYNE

In 1688, the Catholic King of England, James II, was deposed from his throne, to be replaced by his Protestant daughter, Mary, and her husband, William of Orange. Determined to win back the crown, James sought the support of Irish Catholics, and challenged William at Oldbridge by the River Boyne west of Drogheda. The Battle of the Boyne took place on 12 July 1690, with James's poorly trained force of 25,000 French and Irish Catholics facing William's hardened army of 36,000 French Huguenots, Dutch, English and Scots. The Protestants triumphed and James fled to France, after a battle that signalled the beginning of total Protestant power over Ireland. It ushered in the confiscation of Catholic lands and the suppression of Catholic interests, sealing the country's fate for the next 300 years.

William of Orange leading his troops at the Battle of the Boyne, 12 July 1690

their hands before meals. Four of the building's original eight sides survive, each with a graceful Romanesque arch. On the eastern side of the cloister stands the 14th-century chapter house. It has an impressive vaulted ceiling and a floor laid with glazed medieval tiles taken from the abbey church.

The Boyne Valley ㉓

Co Meath. 🚌 to Drogheda.
🚌 to Slane or Drogheda. 🏛 Brú na Bóinne interpretive centre, 041 9880300. ◔ 9:30am–5:30pm (May–Sep: to 6:30pm; Nov–Feb: to 5pm). **www**.heritageireland.ie

Known as Brú na Bóinne, the "Palace of the Boyne", this river valley was the cradle of Irish civilization. The fertile soil supported a sophisticated society in Neolithic times. Much evidence survives, in the form of ring forts, passage graves and sacred enclosures. The most important Neolithic monuments in the valley are three passage graves: supreme among these is **Newgrange** (see pp120–21), but **Dowth** and **Knowth** are significant too. The Boyne Valley also encompasses the Hill of Slane and the Hill of Tara (see p122), both major sites in Celtic lore.

With monuments pre-dating Egypt's pyramids, the Boyne Valley has been dubbed the Irish "Valley of the Kings".

Knowth and Newgrange can only be seen on a tour run by the interpretive centre near Newgrange, which also details the area's Stone Age heritage.

⋔ Dowth
Off N51, 3 km (2 miles) E of Newgrange. ◉ to the public.
This passage grave was plundered in Victorian times by souvenir hunters and has not been fully excavated since. Visitors cannot approach the tomb, but may walk around the outside of the monument.

⋔ Knowth
1.5 km (1 mile) NW of Newgrange. ◔ as Newgrange (see pp120–21). Knowth outdoes Newgrange in several respects, above all in the quantity of its treasures – Europe's greatest concentration of megalithic art. In addition, the site was occupied for a much longer period – from Neolithic times to about 1400.

Unusually, Knowth has two passage tombs rather than one. The excavations begun in 1962 are now complete and the site is open. The tombs can only be viewed externally to prevent further decay and visitors must sign up for tours via Brú na Bóinne (see p120).

River Boyne near the site of the Battle of the Boyne

Newgrange ㉔

Tri-spiral carving in chamber

The origins of Newgrange, one of the most important passage graves in Europe, are steeped in mystery. According to Celtic lore, the legendary kings of Tara *(see p122)* were buried here, but Newgrange predates them. Built in around 3200 BC, the grave was left untouched by all invaders (though not by tomb robbers) and was eventually excavated in the 1960s. Archaeologists then discovered that on the winter solstice (21 December), rays of sun enter the tomb and light up the burial chamber – making it the oldest solar observatory in the world. All visitors to Newgrange and Knowth are admitted through the visitors' centre *(see p119)* from where tours of the historic sight are taken; early arrival is advised in summer to avoid long queues.

Basin stone
The chiselled stones, found in each recess, would have once contained funerary offerings and the bones of the dead.

The chamber has three recesses or side chambers: the north recess is the one struck by sunlight on the winter solstice.

Chamber ceiling
The burial chamber's intricate corbelled ceiling, which reaches a height of 6 m (20 ft) above the floor, has survived intact. The overlapping slabs form a conical hollow, topped by a single capstone.

CONSTRUCTION OF NEWGRANGE

The tomb at Newgrange was designed by people with clearly exceptional artistic and engineering skills, who had use of neither the wheel nor metal tools. About 200,000 tonnes of loose stones were transported to build the mound, or cairn, which protects the passage grave. Larger slabs were used to make the circle around the cairn (12 out of a probable 35 stones have survived), the kerb and the tomb itself. Many of the kerbstones and the slabs lining the passage, the chamber and its recesses are decorated with zigzags, spirals and other geometric motifs. The grave's corbelled ceiling consists of smaller, unadorned slabs and has proved almost completely waterproof for the last 5,000 years.

Mound

Entrance

Stone circle (existing stones shaded)

100 m
328 ft

Decorated stones (shaded)

Recesses   Passage   Entrance

25 m
82 ft

Plan of passage and burial chamber

VISITORS' CHECKLIST

8 km (5 miles) E of Slane, Co
Meath. **Tel** 041 9880300. 🚍 to
Drogheda. 🚍 to Drogheda &
Drogheda to visitor's centre. 🕐
mid-Sep–May: 9:30am–6:30pm
daily (Oct, Mar, Apr: to 5:30pm;
Nov–Feb: to 5pm); Jun–mid-Sep:
9am–7pm daily. ⬤ 24–27 Dec.
📷 🚫 inside. 📹 obligatory (last
tour: 1 hr 45 min before closing).
🎫 www.heritageireland.ie

Restoration of Newgrange

*Located on a low ridge north of the Boyne, Newgrange
took more than 70 years to build. Between 1962
and 1975 the passage grave and mound were
restored as closely as possible to their original state.*

The standing stones in
the passage are slabs of
slate which would have
been collected locally.

Passage

*At dawn on 21
December, a beam of
sunlight shines through
the roof box (a feature
unique to Newgrange),
travels along the 19-m
(62-ft) passage and hits
the central recess in the
burial chamber.*

**The retaining
wall** around the
front of the cairn
was rebuilt using
the white quartz
and granite
stones found
scattered around
the site during
excavations.

Roof box

Entrance

*Newgrange's most elaborately
carved kerbstone stands just
in front of the entrance,
forming part of the kerb of
huge slabs around the cairn.*

Trim Castle, set in water meadows beside the River Boyne

Slane 25

Co Meath. 950. 041 988 0305. www.eastcoastmidlands.ie

Slane is an attractive estate village, centred on a quartet of Georgian houses. The Boyne river flows through it and skirts around **Slane Castle Demesne**, set in glorious grounds laid out in the 18th century by the renowned landscape gardener, Capability Brown. The castle, dating from 1785, incorporates the designs of James Wyatt, Francis Johnson and James Gandon and is famous for its Gothic Revival ballroom designed by Thomas Hopper. The castle was badly damaged by fire in 1991 but reopened in 2001 after a decade of restoration. Just to the north rises the **Hill of Slane** where, in AD 433, St Patrick is said to

have lit a Paschal (Easter) fire as a challenge to the pagan High King of Tara. The local priest still marks this event by the lighting of a fire at Easter.

Hill of Tara 26

Nr Killmessan Village, Co Meath. **Tel** May–Oct: 046 25903; Nov–Apr: Brú na Bóinne 041 9880300. to Navan. May–Oct: 10am–6pm daily (last adm: 5:15pm). for interpretive centre. www.heritageireland.ie

A site of mythic importance, Tara was the political and spiritual centre of Celtic Ireland and the seat of the High Kings until the 11th century. The spread of Christianity, which eroded the importance of Tara, is marked by a statue of St Patrick. Tara's symbolism was not lost on Daniel O'Connell (*see p16),* who chose the site

for a rally in 1843, attended by more than a million people.

Tours from the interpretive centre point out a Stone Age passage grave and Iron Age hill forts though, to the untutored eye, these look like mere hollows and grassy mounds. Clearest is the Royal Enclosure, an oval fort, in the centre of which is Cormac's House containing the "stone of destiny" *(Liath Fáil),* an ancient fertility symbol and inauguration stone of the High Kings. However, all this is secondary to the views over the Boyne Valley and the site's sense of history.

Trim 27

Co Meath. 6,500. Mill St, 046 9437111. Fri. www.eastcoastmidlandsireland.ie

Trim is one of the most pleasing Midlands market towns. A Norman stronghold on the River Boyne, it marked a boundary of the Pale *(see p108).* Trim runs efficient heritage and genealogy centres, including a visitors' centre next door to the tourist office.

Trim Castle was founded in 1173 by Hugh de Lacy, a Norman knight, and is one of the largest medieval castles in Europe. It makes a spectacular backdrop so is often used as a film set, most recently seen in Mel Gibson's *Braveheart* (1995). The castle is currently closed for renovation, but visitors can peer in from a barbican tower that is still open. In the summer, the Nun Run, a bizarre horse race with nuns as jockeys, takes place near the castle.

Aerial view of Iron Age forts on the Hill of Tara

Over the river is **Talbot Castle**, an Augustinian abbey converted to a manor house in the 15th century. Just north of the abbey, **St Patrick's Cathedral** incorporates part of a medieval church with a 15th-century tower and sections of the original chancel.

Butterstream Gardens, on the edge of town, are the best in the county. A luxuriant herbaceous bed is the centrepiece, but equally pleasing are the woodland, rose and white gardens. The design is enhanced by pergolas, pools and bridges.

🌼 **Butterstream Gardens**
Kildalkey Rd. **Tel** 046 9436017.
☐ Apr–Sep: 11am–6pm daily. 🏷

Lighting votive candles in Mullingar Cathedral

Mullingar 28

Co Westmeath. 🏠 14,000. 🚌 🚆
ℹ Market Sq, 044 9348650. 🛒 Sat.

The county town of Westmeath is a prosperous market town encircled by the Royal Canal (see p85), which links Dublin with the River Shannon. Although Mullingar's main appeal is as a base to explore the surrounding area, pubs such as Con's and cheery Canton Casey's can make a pleasant interlude. In addition, the 20th-century cathedral features unusual mosaics of St Anne and St Patrick.

Environs
Recent restoration of the Dublin to Mullingar stretch of the Royal Canal has resulted in attractive towpaths for canalside walks, as well as good

The remains of the Jealous Wall at Belvedere House, near Mullingar

angling facilities. South of Mullingar, just off the road to Kilbeggan, stands **Belvedere House**, a romantic Palladian villa overlooking Lough Ennel. Built in 1740 by architect Richard Castle, Belvedere is decorated with Rococo plasterwork and set in wonderful gardens. Shortly after the house was built, the first Earl of Belvedere accused his wife of having an affair with his brother, and imprisoned her for 31 years in a neighbouring house. He sued the brother and had him jailed for life. In 1760, the Earl built a Gothic folly – the Jealous Wall – in order to block the view from another brother's more opulent mansion. The Jealous Wall still remains, as does an octagonal gazebo and other follies.

Miniature whiskey bottles at Locke's Distillery in Kilbeggan

Charming terraces, framed by urns and yews, descend to the lake; on the other side of the house is a pretty walled garden, enclosed by an arboretum and rolling parkland. There is also an animal sanctuary next to the visitor centre.

🏛 **Belvedere House**
6 km (4 miles) S of Mullingar. **Tel** 044 9349060. **Gardens** ☐ daily. May, Apr, Sep–Feb: 10:30am–7pm (Nov–Feb: to 4:30pm); May–Aug: 9:30am–9pm (last adm: 1hr before closing). 🏷 ☐ of estate by tram. ♿ visitor centre only.
☐ 🚻 **www**.belvedere-house.ie

Kilbeggan 29

Co Westmeath. 🏠 600. 🚌

Situated between Mullingar and Tullamore, this pleasant village has a small harbour on the Grand Canal. However, the main point of interest is **Locke's Distillery**. Founded in 1757, it claims to be the oldest licensed pot still distillery in the world. Unable to compete with Scotch whisky manufacturers, the company went bankrupt in 1954, but the aroma hung in the warehouses for years and was known as "the angels' share". The distillery was reopened as a museum in 1987. The building is authentic, a solid structure complete with a water wheel and an indoor steam engine. A tour traces the process of Irish whiskeymaking, from the mash tuns through to the fermentation vats and creation of wash (rough beer) to the distillation and maturation stages. At the tasting stage, workers would sample the whiskey in the can pit room. Visitors can still taste whiskeys in the bar but, unlike the original workers, cannot bathe in the whiskey vats.

🏛 **Locke's Distillery**
Museum Main St. **Tel** 057 9332134.
☐ Apr–Oct: 9am–6pm daily; Nov–Mar: 10am–4pm daily. 🏷 🍴
www.lockesdistillerymuseum.com

TRAVELLERS'
NEEDS

WHERE TO STAY

Whether you are staying in exclusive luxury or modest bed-and-breakfast accommodation, one thing you can be certain of in Dublin is that you will receive a warm welcome. The Irish are renowned for their friendliness and even in big corporate hotels, where you might expect the reception to be more impersonal, the staff go out of their way to be hospitable. The choice is enormous: you can stay in an elegant, refurbished Georgian house, a comfortable bed-and-breakfast, a Victorian

Doorman at the Conrad Hotel

townhouse, an old-fashioned commercial hotel or a cosy pub. Details are given here of the various types of accommodation available. The listings on pages 128–33 recommend around 60 hotels in both central Dublin and outside the city – all places of quality, ranging from basic to luxury – and should help you decide upon your choice of accommodation. Fáilte Ireland (the Irish Tourist Board) and Dublin Tourism also publish comprehensive guides to recommended accommodation in the area.

Main entrance to the fashionable Clarence Hotel (see p131)

HOTELS

At the top of the price range there are quite a few expensive, luxury hotels in the heart of Dublin. Magnificently furnished and run, they offer maximum comfort, delicious food and often have indoor facilities, such as a gym and swimming pool. As well as luxurious individual hotels there are also the modern hotel chains, such as **Bewleys** and **Irish Welcome**, which offer a high standard of accommodation. However, these establishments can lack the charm and individuality of privately run hotels.

There are also numerous very moderate hotels in the centre of Dublin, providing a good standard of accommodation.

If you prefer to stay outside Dublin, there are some wonderful castles and stately homes which offer the same standards as the top city hotels but which have the bonus of being set in beautiful countryside. They can often also arrange outdoor pursuits such as fishing, riding and golf.

The shamrock symbol of **Fáilte Ireland** is displayed by hotels (and other forms of accommodation) that have been inspected and approved.

BED-AND-BREAKFAST ACCOMMODATION

Ireland has a reputation for the best B&Bs in Europe. Your welcome will always be friendly and the food and company excellent. Even if the house is no architectural

The entrance to the grand Shelbourne Hotel (see p130) on St Stephen's Green

A contemporary deluxe bedroom in the Brooks Hotel (see p130)

beauty, the comfort and atmosphere will more than compensate. Not all of the bedrooms have bathrooms *en suite*. When one is available, you may possibly have to pay a little extra but, considering the generally cheap rates, the surcharge is negligible.

The Irish swear by their B&Bs and many stay in them by choice rather than paying to stay in the luxurious surroundings of some of the big hotels. **Town and Country Homes** will provide details of bed-and-breakfast accommodation throughout Ireland.

GUESTHOUSES

Most guesthouses are found in cities and large towns. They are usually converted family homes and have an atmosphere all of their own. Most offer a good-value evening meal and all give you a delicious full Irish breakfast (see p136). Top-of-the-range guesthouses can be just as good, and sometimes even better, than hotels. You will see a much more personal side of a town or city while

◁ View of Ha'Penny Bridge from O'Connell Bridge

staying at a guesthouse. There are plenty to choose from in the Dublin area and the prices are usually reasonable. The **Irish Hotels Federation** publishes a useful booklet with guesthouse listings that cover the whole of Ireland, including Dublin and its environs.

PRICES

Room rates advertised are inclusive of service and tax. Hotel rates can vary by as much as 40 per cent depending on the time of year. Prices in guesthouses are influenced more by their proximity to tourist sights and public transport. Dublin offers a complete range of accommodation, from youth hostels through very reasonably priced bed-and-breakfasts to lavish five-star hotels such as the Merrion, Morrison and the Clarence.

TIPPING

Tipping in Dublin is a matter of personal discretion but is not common practice, even at the larger hotels. Tasks performed by staff are considered part of the service. Tipping is not expected for carrying bags to your room or for serving drinks. However, it is usual to tip the waiting staff in hotel restaurants: the standard tip is around 10–15 per cent of the bill – anything in excess of that would be considered particularly generous.

The elegant and modern reception at The Morrison hotel *(see p131)*

BOOKING

It is wise to reserve your accommodation during the peak season and public holidays *(see p29)*, particularly if your visit coincides with a local festival such as the St Patrick's Day celebrations *(see p26)* when the city can get booked up. **Dublin Tourism** *(see p164)* can offer advice and make reservations through its accommodation service. Central reservation facilities are available at the hotel chains listed here.

YOUTH HOSTELS

There are 31 youth hostels registered with **An Óige** (the Irish Youth Hostel Association), with one in the Dublin area. Accommodation is provided in dormitories with

Fáilte Ireland accommodation sign

comfortable beds and basic cooking facilities. You can only use these hostels if you are a member of An Óige or another organization affiliated to the International Youth Hostel Federation.

There are also independent hostels, and places such as universities that offer similar inexpensive accommodation in Dublin. The tourist board has listings of those places that are recommended.

DISABLED TRAVELLERS

A fact sheet for disabled visitors is produced by Fáilte Ireland and their accommodation guide indicates wheelchair accessibility. Dublin Tourism and **Comhairle** are also helpful. *Accommodation for Disabled Persons* and *Dublin: A Guide for Disabled Persons* are useful leaflets which are available at the tourist office.

The stately charm of Dunbrody Country House *(see p133)*

Choosing a Hotel

The hotels in this guide have been selected across a wide price range for their good value, facilities and location. These listings highlight some of the factors that may influence your choice. Hotels are listed by area, beginning with the Southeast. For information on restaurants in the area, see pages 138–145.

PRICE CATEGORIES
For a standard double room per night, including tax, service charges and breakfast.

€ Under 120 euros
€€ 120–160 euros
€€€ 160–190 euros
€€€€ 190–250 euros
€€€€€ Over 250 euros

SOUTHEAST DUBLIN

Davenport
€€

Merrion Square, Dublin 2 **Tel** *01 607 3500* **Fax** *01 661 5663* **Rooms** *114*
     Map *F4*

This hotel lies in the heart of Georgian Dublin, and its Neo-Classical façade dates from 1863. Mahogany, brass and marble furnishings give the Davenport the feel of a gentleman's club. The ample bedrooms are well appointed, with a warmly coloured decor. A fitness suite and a business centre are available. **www.ocallaghanhotels.ie**

Harcourt Hotel
€€

60 Harcourt Street, Dublin 2 **Tel** *01 478 3677* **Fax** *01 475 2013* **Rooms** *104*
     Map *D5*

Just off St Stephen's Green, the Harcourt boasts a beautifully central location. Although the interior is fairly unremarkable, bedrooms are modern and well equipped. A popular nightclub, D-Two, is situated in the basement of the hotel and is a draw for late-night revellers. **www.harcourthotel.ie**

Kilronan House
€€

70 Adelaide Road, Dublin 2 **Tel** *01 475 5266* **Fax** *01 478 2841* **Rooms** *15*

Situated on a leafy street near St Stephen's Green, around the corner from the National Concert Hall, this listed townhouse dates back to 1834. Although it retains its Georgian character, it is newly refurbished with all modern comforts, including orthopaedic beds. Delicious breakfasts and friendly hosts. **www.dublinn.com**

Leeson Hotel
€€

27 Leeson Street Lower, Dublin 2 **Tel** *01 676 3380* **Fax** *01 661 8273* **Rooms** *20*
     Map *E5*

Close to St Stephen's Green, this cheerfully decorated hotel is spread across two Georgian buildings. The ambience is relaxed and informal, but the service is of a high quality. The hotel bar, Kobra, is elegant, with wood furnishings. Bedrooms are tidy and comfortable, if somewhat on the small side. **www.theleesonhotel.com**

Longfields
€€

10 Fitzwilliam Street Lower, Dublin 2 **Tel** *01 676 1367* **Fax** *01 676 1542* **Rooms** *26*
     Map *F5*

Two interconnected Georgian buildings make up this small, stylish hotel, situated between the appealing Fitzwilliam and Merrion squares. Furnished with antiques and tasteful reproduction pieces, Longfields exudes the warmth of a private home. Rooms have an individual character, and there is a good restaurant on site. **www.longfields.ie**

Russell Court
€€

21–25 Harcourt Street, Dublin 2 **Tel** *01 478 4066* **Fax** *01 478 4994* **Rooms** *46*
     Map *D5*

Lively and welcoming, the Russell Court is a good choice for younger visitors. The hotel's main attraction lies in its upbeat nightclubs: Bojangles for the 30-plus set and Krystle for a younger crowd. At the rear, Dicey's Garden is a popular beer garden. Bedrooms are neat and tidy, and trams stop near the front. **www.russellcourthotel.ie**

Temple Bar Hotel
€€

Fleet Street, Dublin 2 **Tel** *01 677 3333* **Fax** *01 677 3088* **Rooms** *129*
     Map *D3*

Its location in the heart of Temple Bar – a lively area with several pubs and restaurants – makes this modern hotel popular for stag and hen parties. Bedrooms are clean and adequate, if a little on the small side and lacking in character. A multi-storey car park is available nearby. **www.dublin-hotels.com**

Harrington Hall Guesthouse
€€€

70 Harcourt Street, Dublin 2 **Tel** *475 3497* **Fax** *475 4544* **Rooms** *28*
     Map *D5*

Just off St Stephen's Green, this hotel is housed in two adjoining Georgian buildings. Careful restoration has retained many original features, including high ornamental ceilings and marble bathrooms. Guests can relax in the elegant drawing room, which has an open fire and comfy armchairs. Good breakfast. **www.harringtonhall.com**

Molesworth Court Suites
€€€

Molesworth Court, Schoolhouse Lane, Dublin 2 **Tel** *01 676 4799* **Fax** *01 676 4982* **Rooms** *12*
     Map *E4*

Tucked away in a quiet lane off Molesworth Street, this four-star hotel comprises 12 self-contained apartments and penthouses. Equipped with modern conveniences, the lodgings are stylish and cosy, making this establishment ideal for businesspeople and families alike. Enclosed parking is provided. **www.molesworthcourt.ie**

Key to Symbols *see back cover flap*

Quality Hotel

Sir John Rogerson's Quay, Cardiff Lane, Dublin 2 **Tel** *643 9500* **Fax** *643 9510* **Rooms** *213*

Located in a modern building in the Docklands, the Quality is part of the Choice Hotels chain. Its leisure centre offers a pool, sauna and spa therapies. Rooms are clean, modern and spacious. The hotel's affordability makes up for the 15-minute walk into city centre. **www.qualityhoteldublincity.com**

Stauntons on the Green

83 St Stephen's Green, Dublin 2 **Tel** *01 478 2300* **Fax** *01 478 2263* **Rooms** *57*   **Map** *D5*

Located beside the Ministry of Foreign Affairs, this guesthouse offers comfortable and modest accommodation in three terraced Georgian houses. While bedrooms are reasonably equipped and en suite, those to the rear are quieter, with views of the private garden and Iveagh Gardens. Valet parking is available. **www.dublincityrooms.com**

Trinity Lodge

12 South Frederick Street, Dublin 2 **Tel** *01 617 0900* **Fax** *01 617 0999* **Rooms** *16*   **Map** *E4*

Close to Grafton Street and Trinity College, this Georgian townhouse enjoys one of the best locations in town. Though traditional in style, it is furnished with all modern conveniences, and the warmly coloured en-suite bedrooms are well maintained. Spend some time at Georges, the in-house bistro. **www.trinitylodge.com**

Mont Clare

Merrion Square, Dublin 2 **Tel** *01 607 3800* **Fax** *01 661 5663* **Rooms** *80*   **Map** *F4*

Though not as grand as its sister hotel the Davenport *(see p128)*, Mont Clare is traditionally furnished in mahogany and brass. The well-appointed bedrooms are air conditioned and tastefully decorated. The sizeable and popular bar serves carvery lunches. Guests may use the gym across the road. **www.ocallaghanhotels.ie**

Morgan Hotel

10 Fleet Street, Dublin 2 **Tel** *01 643 7000* **Fax** *01 643 7060* **Rooms** *121*   **Map** *D3*

In the heart of Temple Bar, this self-styled boutique hotel is contemporary in design, with clean lines and uncluttered public spaces. The minimalistic bedrooms have beech furnishings, cotton linen and CD systems. The ambience is relaxing, though the rooms overlooking the street can be noisy. There is a fine bar on site. **www.themorgan.com**

St Stephen's Green Hotel

St Stephen's Green, Dublin 2 **Tel** *01 607 3600* **Fax** *01 661 5663* **Rooms** *74*   **Map** *D4*

Warm and friendly, this hotel is superbly located on the southwest corner of St Stephen's Green. It consists of two splendid Georgian townhouses with a modern glass atrium. The spacious bedrooms are clean and well equipped, with comfortable beds and nice views of the green. **www.ocallaghanhotels.com**

Stephen's Hall Hotel

14–17 Leeson Street Lower, Dublin 2 **Tel** *01 638 1111* **Fax** *01 638 1122* **Rooms** *30*   **Map** *E5*

Situated close to St Stephen's Green, the recently refurbished Stephen's Hall provides suites that include an attached kitchen. Its proximity to the vibrant city centre makes this hotel a very good value family option. Underground parking is available. **www.stephens-hall.com**

Alexander Hotel

Fenian Street, off Merrion Square, Dublin 2 **Tel** *607 3700* **Fax** *661 5663* **Rooms** *102*   **Map** *F4*

Located beside the National Gallery, the Alexander is a recent build that is tastefully sympathetic to the Georgian surroundings of Merrion Square. Modern rooms have climate control, wireless internet access and large beds. Residents can use the facilities of three sister hotels nearby. **www.ocallaghanhotels.com**

Browne's

22 St Stephen's Green, Dublin 2 **Tel** *01 638 3939* **Fax** *01 638 3900* **Rooms** *11*   **Map** *D4*

Set in a Georgian house overlooking St Stephen's Green, this charming and intimate boutique hotel is stylishly furnished with antiques and quality reproduction pieces. Each of the bedrooms is individually designed with comfort and character in mind. The sophisticated Browne's restaurant serves outstanding food. **www.brownesdublin.com**

Buswell's

25 Molesworth Street, Dublin 2 **Tel** *01 614 6500* **Fax** *01 676 2090* **Rooms** *67*   **Map** *E4*

Comprising five Georgian townhouses, this slightly old-fashioned hotel has been in operation since 1882. It is frequented by political figures, perhaps due to its location beside the government buildings, on a street renowned for commercial art galleries. The sophisticated interior is decorated in warm colours. **www.quinnhotels.com**

Conrad Hotel

Earlsfort Terrace, Dublin 2 **Tel** *01 602 8900* **Fax** *01 676 5424* **Rooms** *192*   **Map** *D5*

Opposite the National Concert Hall, this international-style hotel is geared towards business people. The decor is tasteful and the atmosphere airy. Bedrooms are fitted out in a contemporary style with light wood furnishings and comfortable beds. The higher floors have good views. Professional service. **www.conraddublin.com**

Fitzwilliam Hotel

St Stephen's Green, Dublin 2 **Tel** *478 7000* **Fax** *478 7878* **Rooms** *139*   **Map** *D4*

This five-star hotel features a fresh contemporary design by Sir Terence Conran, including a glass drawbridge in the entrance hall. Rooms are modern and unfussy, except for the penthouse, which boasts a grand piano. Voted one of the Top 20 Hottest Hotels in the World by *Condé Nast Traveller* magazine. **www.fitzwilliamhotel.com**

Merrion

Merrion Street Upper, Dublin 2 **Tel** *01 603 0600* **Fax** *01 603 0700* **Rooms** *142*   **Map** *E4*

In the heart of Georgian Dublin, the Merrion is an elegant and stylish oasis, with open log fires, opulent interiors and a collection of Irish art and antiques. It is a landmark hotel, comprising four listed townhouses from the 1760s, all sensitively restored to their original grandeur. Guests can use the excellent Tethra Spa. **www.merrionhotel.ie**

Number 31

31 Leeson Close, Leeson Street Lower, Dublin 2 **Tel** *01 676 5011* **Fax** *01 676 2929* **Rooms** *21*   **Map** *E5*

Reputedly the most stylish guesthouse in the city, this elegant Georgian establishment is more of a boutique hotel than a B&B, with individually decorated, luxurious bedrooms. The Coach House features a collection of original art and a sunken seating area. Delicious breakfasts are served in the plant-filled conservatory. **www.number31.ie**

Shelbourne Hotel

27 St Stephen's Green, Dublin 2 **Tel** *01 663 4500* **Fax** *01 661 6006* **Rooms** *190*   **Map** *D4*

The five-star Shelbourne, part of the Marriott empire, has been the city's most distinguished hotel since it first opened in 1824. Now extensively restored, the Shelbourne remains a haven of sophistication, featuring Egyptian-cotton bedding, flat-screen TVs and marble bathrooms. **www.marriott.co.uk**

Westbury Hotel

Grafton Street, Dublin 2 **Tel** *01 679 1122* **Fax** *01 679 7078* **Rooms** *205*   **Map** *D4*

Enjoying possibly the most convenient location in the city, the Westbury is only seconds from Dublin's main shopping street. The first floor lobby of this smart, ritzy, yet traditionally styled hotel, is a popular meeting place for afternoon tea. Underground parking comes with free valet service. There is also a small gymnasium. **www.jurysdoyle.com**

Westin Hotel

College Green, Dublin 2 **Tel** *01 645 1000* **Fax** *01 645 1234* **Rooms** *163*   **Map** *D3*

Two 19th-century landmark buildings and part of the former Allied Irish Bank were reconstructed to create this sizeable hotel, across the street from Trinity College. The well-appointed bedrooms are furnished to a high standard; the beds are particularly comfortable. The former vaults of the bank are now a bar, The Mint. **www.westin.com**

SOUTHWEST DUBLIN

Avalon House

55 Aungier Street, Dublin 2 **Tel** *01 475 0001* **Fax** *01 475 0303* **Rooms** *70*   **Map** *C4*

One of the longest established hostels in the city, the centrally located Avalon House provides cheap and cheerful accommodation in a restored red brick Victorian building. Rooms are clean, with pine and tile floors, high ceilings and an open fire. Popular with young travellers, Avalon House also has a café. **www.avalon-house.ie**

Barnacles Hostel

Temple Lane, Temple Bar, Dublin 2 **Tel** *01 671 6277* **Fax** *01 671 6591* **Rooms** *32*   **Map** *C3*

Directly in the middle of Temple Bar, this award-winning hostel is bright, spacious, lively and clean, with a sunny lounge and a self-catering kitchen. There is a variety of rooms, including doubles, twins and dormitories sleeping from four to 12 people. All rooms are en suite. Staff are friendly and helpful. Open 24 hours. **www.barnacles.ie**

Blooms Hotel

Anglesea Street, Dublin 2 **Tel** *01 671 5622* **Fax** *01 671 5997* **Rooms** *97*   **Map** *D3*

The location – on the fringes of Temple Bar and close to Trinity College – is the main selling point of the Blooms. The hotel has an appealing modern exterior, and its compact bedrooms are adequate, if bland – the ones at the front are preferable. There is live music in the busy Vat House Bar, while Club M is a popular nightclub. **www.blooms.ie**

Central Hotel

1–5 Exchequer Street, Dublin 2 **Tel** *01 679 7302* **Fax** *01 679 7303* **Rooms** *70*   **Map** *D5*

Established in 1887, this three-star hotel is aptly named, given its convenient location, very close to Grafton Street. Recently refurbished with modern facilities, the Central retains a somewhat old-fashioned atmosphere, with traditional yet cosy decor. Bedrooms are neat, functional and reasonably priced. **www.centralhotel.ie**

Jury's Inn Christchurch

Christchurch Place, Dublin 8 **Tel** *01 454 0000* **Fax** *01 454 0012* **Rooms** *182*   **Map** *B4*

Opposite Christ Church Cathedral, in the old Viking centre of Dublin, this modern hotel lies within easy walking distance of the Temple Bar area. Rooms are neat and well equipped. Bathrooms are adequate, if a little on the small side. Prices per room are particularly good value for families. **www.jurysdoyle.com**

Brooks

59–62 Drury Street, Dublin 2 **Tel** *01 670 4000* **Fax** *01 670 4455* **Rooms** *98*   **Map** *D4*

This immaculately maintained boutique hotel, located just minutes from Grafton Street, has a club-like feel and a welcoming ambience. It was built in 1997 and remodelled in 2003 with contemporary flourishes and warm colours, though the decor is tastefully traditional. Brooks enjoys a great reputation. **www.brookshotel.com**

Key to Price Guide *see p128* **Key to Symbols** *see back cover flap*

Mercer Hotel

€€€€ Map C5

Lower Mercer Street, Dublin 2 **Tel** *01 478 2179* **Fax** *01 672 9926* **Rooms** *41*

Well located in the city centre, this three-star hotel combines the traditional with the contemporary, as witnessed in its wooden floors, subtle colour scheme and modern furnishings. Bedrooms are clean and comfortable and include all modern conveniences. There is a newly refurbished bar, as well as a restaurant, Cusacks. **www.mercerhotel.ie**

Clarence Hotel

€€€€€ Map C3

6–8 Wellington Quay, Dublin 2 **Tel** *01 407 0800* **Fax** *01 407 0820* **Rooms** *49*

Overlooking the Liffey, this 1852 Dublin landmark was bought by the rock band U2 in 1992. Extensively refurbished, it has now acquired cult status. With original wood panelling in the Arts and Crafts style, and luxuriously furnished rooms, this establishment successfully combines contemporary cool and old-style comfort. **www.theclarence.ie**

NORTH OF THE LIFFEY

Clifden Guest House

€

32 Gardiners Place, Dublin 1 **Tel** *01 874 6364* **Fax** *01 874 6122* **Rooms** *15*

This three-star family-run guesthouse is set in a four-storey Georgian townhouse, just a few minutes' walk from the centre of the city. The high-ceilinged rooms are functional, yet comfortably furnished and cheerfully decorated. They come in varying sizes – one accommodating up to five people. **www.clifdenhouse.com**

Harvey's Hotel

€

11 Upper Gardiner Street, Dublin 1 **Tel** *01 874 8384* **Fax** *01 874 5510* **Rooms** *16*

This hospitable family-run Georgian townhouse, north of the Liffey, is ten minutes' walk from the top of O'Connell Street. Rooms are clean and pleasant; while some are a little jaded, most are nicely decorated. Those at the back are quieter. The atmosphere is friendly and relaxed. **www.harveysguesthouse.com**

Cassidy's Hotel

€€€ Map D2

Cavendish Row, Upper O'Connell Street, Dublin 1 **Tel** *01 878 0555* **Fax** *01 878 0687* **Rooms** *126*

This hotel is conveniently located at the top of O'Connell Street, opposite the Gate Theatre, in three adjoining red brick Georgian townhouses. The generously proportioned rooms have been modernized, but they retain some period features. Spacious bedrooms are all en suite, with contemporary furnishings. **www.cassidyshotel.com**

Clarion IFSC

€€€ Map F2

International Financial Service Centre, North Wall Quay, Dublin 1 **Tel** *01 433 8800* **Rooms** *163*

A short stroll from the centre, the Clarion IFSC offers well-designed and decent accommodation overlooking the River Liffey, in the heart of the financial district. This hotel opened in 2001 and is becoming as popular with tourists as it is with business travellers. Public spaces are bright, airy and minimalist in style. **www.clarionhotelifsc.com**

Gresham Hotel

€€€ Map D1

23 Upper O'Connell Street, Dublin 1 **Tel** *01 874 6881* **Fax** *01 878 7175* **Rooms** *288*

One of Dublin's oldest and best known hotels, the Gresham is a popular rendezvous spot with ever-lively public areas. It has been recently refurbished, with pleasant furnishings that combine classic and contemporary styles. The well-equipped bedrooms are cheerfully decorated. A good business hotel. **www.gresham-hotels.com**

Royal Dublin

€€€€ Map D1

40–42 O'Connell Street, Dublin 2 **Tel** *01 873 3666* **Fax** *01 873 3120* **Rooms** *120*

The modern Royal Dublin is located in one of city's most famous and historic streets. O'Connell Street has been extensively upgraded in recent times, making it much more pleasant than in the past. This hotel may be lacking in atmosphere, but the rooms are self-sufficient. Those at the rear are quieter. Friendly staff. **www.royaldublin.com**

The Morrison

€€€€€ Map C3

Ormond Quay, Dublin 1 **Tel** *01 887 2400* **Fax** *01 878 3185* **Rooms** *138*

Located on the quay overlooking the river, this luxurious hotel was built in 1999, with John Rocha as design consultant. The interior is a mix of high ceilings, dark woods, pale walls, dim lighting, handcrafted Irish carpets and original art. Bedrooms have a modern design. There is also a stylish restaurant, Halo. **www.morrisonhotel.ie**

FURTHER AFIELD

Clara House

€

23 Leinster Road, Rathmines, Dublin 6 **Tel** *01 497 5904* **Fax** *01 497 5580* **Rooms** *13*

Built in 1840, this listed red brick Georgian house is a favoured B&B. It is a 15-minute walk from the city centre, and there is also a good bus route into town. The atmosphere is relaxed and friendly. Secure private car park is available at the rear. The pleasant waterside walks along the canal are an added attraction. **www.clarahouse.com**

Donnybrook Hall €

6 Belmont Avenue, Donnybrook, Dublin 4 **Tel** *01 269 1633* **Fax** *01 269 2649* **Rooms** *9*

This family-run guesthouse is located on a quiet residential street near the Royal Dublin Society showgrounds and Landsdowne Road stadium. The interior is light and elegant, and all rooms have orthopaedic mattresses. Three of them open on to a garden. Great breakfasts include pancakes, French toast and fresh fruit. **www.donnybrookhall.com**

Druid Lodge €

Killiney Hill Road, Killiney, Co Dublin **Tel** *01 285 1632* **Fax** *01 285 8504* **Rooms** *4*

Situated on picturesque Killiney Hill, overlooking the bay, Druid Lodge is 11 km (7 miles) south of Dublin city centre. A charming ivy-clad guesthouse, it was built in 1832 and named after the adjoining sacred site of Druid's Chair. Exuding a peaceful, old-world charm, it is well furnished and comfortable. **www.druidlodge.com**

Glenogra Guesthouse €

64 Merrion Road, Ballsbridge, Dublin 4 **Tel** *01 668 3661* **Fax** *01 668 3698* **Rooms** *12*

This stylish and award-winning guesthouse provides pleasant and good value B&B accommodation in a leafy, upmarket area of Dublin. The owners create a welcoming atmosphere for their guests: bedrooms are pleasantly appointed, and the breakfast is good. **www.glenogra.com**

Marble Hall Guest Accommodation €

81 Marlborough Road, Donnybrook, Dublin 4 **Tel** *01 497 7350* **Rooms** *3*

This much-loved guesthouse is set in a leafy residential area, 20 minutes' walk from town and on a well-serviced bus route. Victorian in style, it is meticulously maintained by Shelagh Conway, who is renowned for her excellent breakfasts. Bedrooms are spacious and tastefully decorated with antique furniture. **www.marblehall.net**

Mount Herbert Hotel €

7 Herbert Road, Ballsbridge, Dublin 4 **Tel** *01 668 4321* **Fax** *01 660 7077* **Rooms** *168*

Established for more than 50 years, the Mount Herbert is located in a residential area close to the Landsdowne Road stadium. It consists of a terrace of interconnecting houses decorated with modern furnishings. The en-suite bedrooms are equipped with good facilities. There is free access to a nearby gym. **www.mountherberthotel.ie**

Tara Towers Hotel €

Merrion Road, Booterstown, Dublin 4 **Tel** *01 269 4666* **Fax** *01 269 1027* **Rooms** *111*

South of the city centre, this three-star hotel is situated on the coastal road. Dun Laoghaire is a 15-minute drive away, and there is a well-serviced bus route and a DART station nearby. The ambience is relaxed, and bedrooms are comfortable and spacious, if rather basic in decor. There is a traditional restaurant on site. **www.taratowers.com**

Belcamp Hutchinson €€

Carrs Lane, Malahide Road, Balgriffin, Dublin 17 **Tel** *01 846 0843* **Fax** *01 848 5703* **Rooms** *8*

Only 15 minutes' drive from the airport, this secluded, creeper-clad Georgian house offers B&B accommodation. The friendly and welcoming hosts and large, high-ceilinged rooms make for a pleasant stay. Nearby, the picturesque seaside village of Malahide offers golf, tennis, sailing and horse-riding facilities. **www.belcamphutchinson.com**

Butlers Town House €€

44 Landsdowne Road, Ballsbridge, Dublin 4 **Tel** *01 667 4022* **Fax** *01 667 3960* **Rooms** *20*

Furnished in a country-house style, this Georgian guesthouse offers four-star accommodation in individually designed bedrooms with Egyptian cotton sheets. Good breakfasts are served in the Conservatory Restaurant, which features an all-day menu, making this more of a small hotel than a B&B. **www.butlers-hotel.com**

Crowne Plaza Hotel €€

Northwood Park, Santry Demesne, Santry, Dublin 9 **Tel** *01 862 8888* **Fax** *01 862 8800* **Rooms** *204*

Set in mature parkland, just five minutes from Dublin Airport and 15 minutes from the city centre, the Crowne Plaza offers all modern comforts. Rooms are well equipped, and there is an on-site fitness centre. A 24-hour courtesy coach for the airport is available. Located close to the M1 and M50 motorways. **www.cpdublin-airport.com**

The Red Bank €€

6–7 Church Street, Skerries, Co Dublin **Tel** *01 849 1005* **Fax** *01 849 1598* **Rooms** *18*

On the premises of a former bank, in the heart of the village of Skerries, this guesthouse offers comfortably furnished rooms with good facilities. The award-winning Red Bank Restaurant has great character and specializes in seafood. Warm hospitality is guaranteed. Dublin Airport is just a short drive away. **www.redbank.ie**

Waterloo House €€

8–10 Waterloo Road, Ballsbridge, Dublin 4 **Tel** *01 660 1888* **Fax** *01 667 1955* **Rooms** *17*

A short walk from St Stephen's Green, this lovely guesthouse comprises two adjoining Georgian buildings on a tree-lined road, away from the bustle of the city. The ambience is informal, and the bedrooms cosy. A good, hearty breakfast is served in a cheerful dining room. Off-street parking is available. **www.waterloohouse.ie**

Berkeley Court Hotel €€€

Landsdowne Road, Ballsbridge, Dublin 4 **Tel** *01 665 3200* **Fax** *01 661 7238* **Rooms** *186*

In the heart of the embassy belt, this five-star hotel is conveniently located for the Royal Dublin Society showground and Landsdowne Road stadium. Beyond the unappealing exterior, the chandeliered lobby sets the tone for a plush ambience. Rooms are well appointed and there are two good restaurants. **www.jurysdoyle.com**

Key to Price Guide *see p128* **Key to Symbols** *see back cover flap*

Grand Canal Hotel

Grand Canal Street, Ballsbridge, Dublin 4 **Tel** *01 646 1000* **Fax** *01 646 1001* **Rooms** *142*

Winner of the New Hotel of the Year award in 2005, the Grand Canal is spacious and modern, with a friendly staff. The on-site pub, Kitty O'Sheas, is one of the best in town. There is also a new restaurant, Epic. It is conveniently located between Trinity College and Landsdowne Road. **www.grandcanalhotel.com**

Herbert Park Hotel

Ballsbridge, Dublin 4 **Tel** *01 667 2200* **Fax** *01 667 2595* **Rooms** *153*

Overlooking the park after which it is named, this big contemporary hotel is bright and airy. Materials used to enliven the interiors include polished granite, Irish abstract art, Irish furniture and glass walls. Bedrooms are well appointed and stylishly designed. **www.herbertparkhotel.ie**

The Burlington

Leeson Street, Dublin 4 **Tel** *01 660 5222* **Fax** *01 660 8496* **Rooms** *506*

This four-star hotel is a genuine Dublin institution at the heart of the city's south side. The rooms are smartly appointed, and there is a choice of two restaurants, The Sussex or The Diplomat. Buck Mulligan's bar has a relaxed atmosphere for an afternoon drink. **www.jurysdoyle.com**

Portmarnock Hotel & Golf Links

Portmarnock, Co Dublin **Tel** *01 846 0611* **Fax** *01 846 2422* **Rooms** *135*

Famous for their Irish whiskey, the Jameson family originally owned this house with a lovely beachside location. Close to Dublin Airport, the Portmarnock is tastefully decorated, with bright public spaces. Rooms are excellently furnished, with views of the sea or the championship golf course. There is also a spa. **www.portmarnock.com**

Dylan

Eastmoreland Place, Dublin 4 **Tel** *01 660 3000* **Fax** *01 660 3005* **Rooms** *44*

Awarded the title of Best New Hotel 2007 by Hospitality Ireland, the Dylan boasts a plush interior with sumptuous rooms, each of which has been individually designed. Dine in the hotel's elegant but informal Still restaurant, or sip cocktails in the Dylan bar. **www.dylan.ie**

Four Seasons

Simmonscourt Road, Ballsbridge, Dublin 4 **Tel** *01 665 4000* **Fax** *01 665 4099* **Rooms** *197*

The luxurious Four Seasons combines period-style elegance with contemporary comfort. The large public spaces are opulently decorated with deep-pile rugs and rich furnishings. Bedrooms are large and lavish, and service is exceptional. The Ice Bar is a magnet for fashionistas. There are also 25 apartments. **www.fourseasons.com**

BEYOND DUBLIN

Beaufort House

Ghan Road, Carlingford, Co Louth **Tel** *042 937 3879* **Rooms** *6*

Michael Caine (not the film star) is a fantastic chef. Along with their core business of sailing courses and yacht charter, he and wife Glynis run this award-winning guesthouse in medieval Carlingford, halfway between Dublin and Belfast. En-suite rooms enjoy sea and mountain views. Great breakfasts. **www.beauforthouse.net**

Smarmore Castle

Ardee, Co Louth **Tel** *041 685 7167* **Fax** *041 685 7650* **Rooms** *5*

This 1320 castle-mansion is a hidden gem. The Mullen family offer a warm welcome and impeccable service, then leave you to enjoy the peaceful garden, rooms – all different – and the drawing room. The spa offers massages, Jacuzzi and sauna. Smarmore Castle is one hour from Dublin, close to Newgrange. **www.smarmorecastle.com**

Castle Leslie Estate

Glaslough, Co Monaghan **Tel** *047 88 100* **Fax** *047 88 256* **Rooms** *35*

Located within a thousand acres of rolling countryside, this castle is owned and run by the colourful Leslie family. The hotel itself is a members' club – to stay there more than once, you have to sign up. Accommodation is in the renovated Hunting Lodge. The Organic Spa and equestrian centre are open to visitors, too. **www.castleleslie.com**

Brooklodge Hotel

Macreddin Village, Co Wicklow **Tel** *0402 36444* **Fax** *0402 36580* **Rooms** *90*

Not so much a hotel as a village complex. Standard rooms have four-poster beds; the suites are even more luxurious. The renowned spa offers a flotation tank and hammam massages. There is also a pub with its own microbrewery, an equestrian centre, an organic food fair on Sundays and live jazz on Saturday nights. **www.brooklodge.com**

Dunbrody Country House Hotel

Arthurstown, Co Wexford **Tel** *051 389 600* **Fax** *051 389 601* **Rooms** *22*

Set in parkland on the dramatic Hook Peninsula, this 1830s Georgian manor offers a relaxing, elegant atmosphere complemented by log fires and a luxury spa. Guests can flavour their spa visit with tasty delicacies designed to be enjoyed in-between treatments. Rooms are individually styled. **www.dunbrodyhouse.com**

RESTAURANTS, CAFES AND PUBS

The Dublin of today is a modern, cosmopolitan city, something which is reflected in its vast array of restaurants. The Temple Bar area is good for modern international cuisine, and also has a large number of pubs as well as a few traditional Irish restaurants. There are many Italian, Chinese and Indian restaurants, and in recent years Thai, Indonesian, Japanese, Mexican and Cuban places have proliferated. Seafood and fish is abundant in

The Bad Ass Café, Temple Bar

Dublin, in particular smoked salmon and oysters; the latter is famously often consumed with Guinness. Popular for a light lunch is smoked salmon on delicious dark rye bread, with a pint of Guinness. Wherever you eat, portions will be generous, especially in pubs, whose platefuls of roast meat and vegetables offer excellent value for money. Takeaway food, from fish and chips to pizzas and kebabs, is also widely available.

IRISH EATING PATTERNS

Traditionally, the Irish have started the day with a huge breakfast: bacon, sausages, black pudding, eggs, tomatoes and brown bread. The main meal, dinner, was served at midday, with a lighter "tea" in the early evening.

Although Continental breakfasts are now available, the traditional breakfast is still included in almost all hotel and B&B rates. Most of the Irish today settle for a light lunch and save their main meal for the evening. Vestiges of the old eating patterns remain in the huge midday meals still served in pubs.

EATING OUT

Elegant dining becomes considerably more affordable when you make lunch your main meal of the day. In many of the top restaurants in Dublin, the fixed-price lunch

and dinner menus offer much the same, but the bill at lunchtime will usually amount to about half the price. If you like wine to accompany your meal, the house wines are quite drinkable in most restaurants and can reduce the total cost of your meal. If you are travelling with children, look out for one of the many restaurants that offer a children's menu. Lunch in Dublin is invariably served between noon and 2:30pm, with dinner between 6:30 and 10pm, although many ethnic and city-centre restaurants stay open later. If you are staying in a bed-and-breakfast, your hosts may provide a home-cooked evening meal if given advance notice. Visa and MasterCard are the most commonly accepted credit cards in Ireland, with American Express and Diners Club also in use.

GOURMET AND ETHNIC DINING

Once considerably lacking in gourmet establishments, Dublin now offers many restaurants that rank among Europe's very best, with chefs trained in outstanding domestic and Continental institutions. Increasingly it is the hotels which house some of the city's best restaurants, with award-winning cuisine. There is a choice of Irish, French, Italian, Chinese, Indian, Cuban, Indonesian, Japanese, Mexican, Thai and even Russian cuisines to be found in and around Dublin. Locations vary as widely as the cuisine, from conventional hotel dining rooms, townhouse basements and city mansions to romantic castle hotels and tiny village cafés tucked away by the sea.

An Irish coffee

In the city centre, the eating areas with the widest choice tend to be located in Temple Bar or between St Stephen's Green and Merrion Square. Outside the city, Malahide and Howth have a good selection of restaurants, and Dun Laoghaire is worth a special visit for fresh fish and seafood.

BUDGET DINING

It is quite possible to eat well on a moderate budget in Dublin. Both in the city and outside it, there are small

The Mermaid Café, with its floor-to-ceiling windows (*see p142*)

La Stampa's luxurious bar, Samsara (see p139)

FISH AND CHIPS AND OTHER FAST FOODS

The Irish, from peasant to parliamentarian, love their "chippers", immortalized in Roddy Doyle's novel *The Van*, and any good pub night will often end with a visit to the nearest fish-and-chip shop. At virtually any time of day, however, if you pass by Leo Burdock's in Dublin, there will be a long queue for this international institution *(see p141)*. With Ireland's long coastline, wherever you choose, the fish will usually be the freshest catch of the day – plaice, cod, haddock, whiting or ray (a delicacy). As an alternative to fish and chips, there are numerous good pasta and pizza restaurants around the city, including the Steps of Rome, Pasta Fresca and Milano, which also does takeaways. In addition Dublin has become home to the ubiquitous burger chains, including McDonald's, as well as other forms of fast food outlets such as KFC.

Picnickers enjoying the sunshine outside at Dublin Zoo (see p81)

cafés, tea rooms and family-style restaurants which offer reasonably priced meals. Sandwiches are usually made with thick, delicious slices of fresh, rather than processed, cheese or meat; salad plates feature chicken, pork, beef and the ever-popular smoked salmon; and hot meals usually come with generous helpings of vegetables, with the beloved potato often showing up in different forms, including roasted and mashed, sometimes all on one plate.

Another cheap alternative is to take picnics when you go out. Farmhouse cheeses and homegrown tomatoes make delicious sandwiches, and the beautiful countryside, fine beaches and breathtaking mountains make ideal locations for a picnic. Phoenix Park and Powerscourt both have their own picnic areas.

Whelan's, renowned for its live music programme (see p155)

PUB FOOD

Ireland's pubs have moved into the food field with a vengeance. In addition to bar snacks (soup, sandwiches and so on), available from noon until late, salads and hot meals are served from midday to 2:30pm. At rock-bottom prices, hot plates all come heaped with mounds of fresh vegetables, potatoes, and good portions of local fish or meat. Particularly good value are the pub carveries that offer a choice of joints, sliced to your preference. In recent years, the international staples of spaghetti, lasagne and quiche have also appeared on pub menus, along with more Mediterranean dishes such as *bruschetta* in the trendier pubs. For a list of recommended pubs, see pages 146–7.

PUB OPENING HOURS

Many people come to Dublin for its endless pubs and bars and its excellent stouts and whiskeys. Opening hours are the same winter and summer alike: Monday to Wednesday 10:30am until 11:30pm; Thursday to Saturday 10:30am until 12:30pm. Sunday opening times have changed to become more flexible. Pubs used to close for "holy hour" between 2pm and 4pm. Now most pubs are open on a Sunday from 12:30pm until 11pm. Late bars tend to stay open until 1am or 2am, the nightclubs even later.

VEGETARIAN FOOD

As with most western European cities, there is plenty of scope for vegetarians to eat well in Dublin. Although much traditional Irish food is meat-based, most restaurants will have vegetarian dishes on the menu, particularly in the modern international and Italian restaurants, but there are also some excellent exclusively vegetarian restaurants in the city. If you happen to go somewhere to eat and realize that there is no vegetarian option, most restaurants will be more than happy to make something up for you, such as a salad or a vegetable stir fry.

The Flavours of Ireland

Boxty, barm brack, champ, coddle, cruibins, colcannon – the
basic dishes that have nourished Ireland are spiced with
fancy names. But the secret of their success is their
ingredients, which are nurtured in a warm, damp
climate on lush hills that brings them flavour. Beef and
dairy cattle can stay out all year and produce abundant
butter, cheese and cream. Pork and pork products, such
as ham and bacon, are a mainstay, though lamb is traditional,
too. Potatoes, the king of vegetables, turn up in soup, pies,
cakes, bread and scones that are piled on breakfast and tea
tables. And the rivers, lakes and shores are rich in seafood.

Oysters

Sea trout, plucked fresh from the
Atlantic Ocean

THE BASIC DISHES

Irish stews are thick and
tasty, traditionally featuring
lamb or mutton, onion and
potatoes, while beef and
Guinness (see pp82–3) make
a darker casserole, some-
times with the addition of
oysters. Carrots and turnips
are the first choice of vegetables. Pork is the basis of
many dishes. Trotters, called

cruibins or crubeens, are
sometimes pickled, while
bacon can be especially
meaty. Dublin coddle, a
fill-me-up after the pub on
a Saturday night, relies on
sausages and potatoes as
well as bacon. Ham is
sometimes smoked over
peat and, for special
occasions, it is baked with
cloves and brown sugar
and served with buttered
cabbage. Cabbage is the
basis of colcannon, with

mashed potato and onions,
sometimes with butter and
milk. Boxty is a bake of
raw and cooked potato
mashed with butter,
buttermilk and flour; champ
is potatoes mashed with
milk, butter and onions.

FISH AND SEAFOOD

The Atlantic Ocean and
Irish Sea have a rich variety
of shellfish, from lobsters
and Dublin Bay prawns to

Barm brack   White soda bread   Brown soda bread   Potato bread

Potato farls   Wheaten bread

Selection of the many traditional Irish breads

TRADITIONAL IRISH FOOD

If your heart is up to it, start
the day with a "Full Irish Fry".
This breakfast fry-up includes
thick, tasty bacon, plus black
pudding, soda farls and potato
cake. A "lady's breakfast" will
have one egg, a "gentleman's"
two. Gooseberry jam will be
spread on fried bread, and
mugs of tea will wash it down.
Irish stews traditionally use mutton,
not so common today, while Spiced
Beef uses up brisket, which is covered in a various spices
then left for a week before being cooked slowly with
Guinness and vegetables. A high tea in the early evening is
the major meal in many homes; a main course will be
followed by a succession of breads and cakes.

Gubbeen cheese

Irish Stew Traditionally,
neck of mutton, potatoes,
carrots and onions are slowly
cooked together for hours.

Delivery in time-honoured style at Moore Street Market, Dublin

mussels and oysters, clams, scallops, and razor-shells. Herring, mackerel, plaice and skate are brought in from the sea, while the rivers and lakes offer up salmon, trout and eels, which are often smoked. Galway salmon and oysters are famous and are served throughout the city's restaurants. Salmon is usually smoked in oak wood kilns. Also traditional is a red seaweed called dulse, mixed with potatoes mashed in their skins to make dulse champ.

BAKED GOODS

Bread and cakes make up a large percentage of the Irish diet. Unleaven soda bread is ubiquitous in both white and brown varieties, and is great with Irish cheeses. Potato bread is fried or eaten cold, as cake. Farls ("quarters") are made with wheat flour or oats, bicarbonate of soda and buttermilk, which goes into many recipes. Fruit breads include barm brack, which is traditionally eaten at Hallowe'en and on All Saint's Day, while rich porter cake is made with Guinness or

A range of Ireland's finest farmhouse cheeses

other stout. White, brown and fruit scones will never be far from tea and breakfast tables.

DAIRY PRODUCTS

Creamy butter, usually salted, is applied generously, on vegetables and in sauces as well as in puddings and on bread. Cream, too, is used in cooking, stirred into soups and whipped for puddings. The variety and quality of Irish farmhouse cheeses has given them a worldwide reputation, and a farmhouse St Killian finally took the crown of "Best Irish Cheese" from Irish Cheddar at the 2007 World Cheese Awards.

IRISH CHEESES

Carrigaline Nutty-tasting, Gouda-like cheese from Cork.

Cashel Blue The only Irish blue cheese. Soft and creamy. Unpasteurized; from Tipperary.

Cooleeny Small, Camembert-style unpasteurized cheese from Tipperary.

Durrus Creamy, natural-rind unpasteurized cheese from West Cork. May be smoked.

Gubbeen Semi-soft washed rind cheese. Rich, milky taste.

Mileens Soft, rich rind-washed cheese. Unpasteurized; from the Beara peninsula, Cork.

St Killian Hexagonal Brie-like creamy cheese from Wexford.

Dublin Coddle *This is a comforting mixture of sausages, bacon, potatoes and onions, stewed in ham stock.*

Galway Salmon *Top quality fish can be simply served with an Irish butter sauce, watercress and colcannon.*

Irish Coffee *This is a chilled soufflé of coffee, cream and Irish whiskey, topped with crushed walnuts.*

Choosing a Restaurant

The restaurants in this guide have been selected across a wide range of price categories for their good value, exceptional food or interesting location. These listings highlight some of the factors that may influence your choice, such as whether you can eat outdoors or if the venue offers live music. Entries are listed by area.

PRICE CATEGORIES
For a three-course evening meal for one including a half bottle of house wine, service and taxes.

€ Under 25 euros
€€ 25–35 euros
€€€ 35–45 euros
€€€€ 45–55 euros
€€€€€ Over 55 euros

SOUTHEAST DUBLIN

Cornucopia
19 Wicklow Street, Dublin 2 **Tel** *01 677 7583*
€
Map *D3*

Small and often crowded, Cornucopia is one of the few exclusively vegetarian restaurants in the city, open for breakfast, lunch and dinner. It serves delicious, cheap and wholesome food – such as salads, soups, pasta dishes, casseroles and quiches – to an army of bookworm bachelors and earthy students.

Nude
21 Suffolk Street, Dublin 2 **Tel** *01 672 5577*
€
Map *D3*

Bono's brother, Norman Hewson, has created a very successful, hip and intimate restaurant that serves freshly prepared food, organic where possible. Soups, panini, wraps, salads and freshly squeezed juices are ordered at the counter. Then, take a seat at the long wooden tables and enjoy these colourful snacks in an upbeat atmosphere.

Steps of Rome
1 Chatham Street, Dublin 2 **Tel** *01 670 5630*
€
Map *D4*

This tiny Italian café, selling great coffee, is always abuzz with people coming and going to collect tasty slices of pizza. The reasonably priced menu includes pasta dishes and bruschettas. Service is brisk, if a little brusque. Steps of Rome is popular with students and fast-moving shoppers pausing for breath. Open all day and into the evening.

Yamamori Noodles
71 South Great George's Street, Dublin 2 **Tel** *01 475 5001*
€
Map *C4*

Very popular with the young crowd, this lively and informal Japanese restaurant specializes in *yamamori ramen* (a noodle dish with meat and vegetables), sushi and sashimi. Try the interesting bento box for variety. Dishes are good value, service is prompt, and the atmosphere is friendly. Evenings are very busy. Open for lunch and dinner.

Avoca Café
11–13 Suffolk Street, Dublin 2 **Tel** *01 672 6019*
€€
Map *D3*

Climb to the top floor of the renowned Irish craft shop Avoca, and you will be rewarded with creative, wholesome and colourful cooking in a bright and airy room. The queues get longer during lunch hour. Such popularity is testament to the delicious salads, panini, hot dishes and wonderful desserts on offer. Open daytime only.

Café Bar Deli
18 South Great George's Street, Dublin 2 **Tel** *01 677 1646*
€€
Map *C4*

Vibrant and modestly priced, Café Bar Deli is decorated in a European café style, with bentwood chairs and a mahogany and brass interior. The imaginative and colourful menus feature pizzas, pasta dishes and salads. Service is prompt and enthusiastic, and the place is particularly popular with 20- and 30-somethings.

Dunne & Cresenzi
14 South Frederick Street, Dublin 2 **Tel** *01 677 3815*
€€
Map *E4*

This delightful Italian wine bar serves authentic food and wine in a stylishly rustic atmosphere. Enjoy the excellent minestrone, antipasti platters, bruschettas, panini, pasta dishes, delicious fruit tartlets and excellent coffee. There is also a superb collection of wines, many of them served by the glass, too. Open all day and into the evening.

Good World Chinese Restaurant
18 South Great George's Street, Dublin 2 **Tel** *01 677 5373*
€€
Map *C4*

This restaurant's popularity with the Chinese community is witness to the superlative and authentic quality of the food on offer. The dim sum selection is a popular choice. Authentic beef, chicken and fish dishes are also on the menu, along with the standard range of Westernized dishes. Friendly and efficient service.

Gotham Café
8 South Anne Street, Dublin 2 **Tel** *01 679 5266*
€€
Map *D4*

Always abuzz with activity, this lively and colourful spot offers bistro-style food at affordable prices. With covers of *Rolling Stone* magazine lining the walls, it is popular with the young – and the young-at-heart. Gotham Café is renowned for its tasty and imaginative pizzas, but it also serves delectable pasta dishes and salads.

Key to Symbols *see back cover flap*

Kilkenny Restaurant and Café

5–6 Nassau Street, Dublin 2 **Tel** *01 677 7075*   **Map** E4

Situated on the first floor of a high quality craft shop, the Kilkenny overlooks the grounds of Trinity College. Wholesome, freshly prepared soups, sandwiches, panini, salads, quiches, hot casseroles and pies are available in this self-service restaurant. Lovely desserts include baked cheesecake, carrot cake and fruit tarts.

La Maison des Gourmets

15 Castle Market, Dublin 2 **Tel** *01 672 7258*   **Map** D4

This boulangerie has a stylish and intimate room upstairs, where high-quality snacks are served. French onion soup, home-baked breads, *tartines* (open sandwiches), salads, a hot special and delicious pastries are on the menu. Takeaway is available from the downstairs shop. In fine weather, you can sit outside and watch the world go by.

The Cedar Tree

118 South Andrew Street, Dublin 2 **Tel** *01 677 2121*   **Map** D3

This restaurant has been serving genuine Lebanese food for almost 20 years. The wide *meze* selection includes hummus, mussels, quails, prawns, baba ganoush, tabbouleh and spiced potatoes. Belly dancing shows take place on Friday and Saturday evenings. The ground floor restaurant, Byblos, serves lighter fare.

Chili Club

Anne's Lane, South Anne Street, Dublin 2 **Tel** *01 677 3721*   **Map** D4

Knock on the door to be let into this award-winning Thai restaurant just off Grafton Street. Do not let the very small, intimate setting and simple decor put you off: the standard of cooking is very high, and the service is great. Thai curries are particularly tasty and the set lunches are good value. AmEx is not accepted.

Ely Wine Bar and Café

22 Ely Place, Dublin 2 **Tel** *01 676 8986*   **Map** E5

Erik and Michelle Robson's unusual wine bar and café, just off St Stephen's Green, has been stylishly converted. The menu features delicious cheese dishes, fish cakes, Kilkee oysters, lamb stew and home-made sausages. The atmosphere is cosy and lively, and the imaginative wine list features some truly exceptional labels.

La Peniche

Grand Canal, Mespil Road, Dublin 4 **Tel** *087 790 00 77*

This floating French/Italian bistro and wine bar is moored on a lovely stretch of the Grand Canal. Each table has an attention light that you can switch on, rather than having to catch the waiter's eye. Every Wednesday and Thursday, cruise dinners are available for an extra 10 euros – be sure to book early. La Peniche can also be chartered privately.

La Stampa

35 Dawson Street, Dublin 2 **Tel** *01 677 4444*   **Map** D4

The main attraction of the brasserie-style La Stampa is its dining room, arguably the most romantic in the city, set in a charming 19th-century mirrored ballroom. Given the food's modest quality, the experience is rather pricey. However, the pleasing ambience and cordial staff more than make up for any shortcomings on your plate.

Pearl Brasserie

20 Merrion Street Upper, Dublin 2 **Tel** *01 661 3572*   **Map** D4

This basement brasserie exudes a cool, contemporary French ethos. It combines charming service with good food at affordable prices. Lunch is particularly good value. Seafood features prominently on the menu, and the impressive wine list is heavy on French labels. The separate Oyster Bar offers lighter fare, including a fish platter.

Trocadero

3–4 St Andrew Street, Dublin 2 **Tel** *01 677 5545*   **Map** D3

This much-loved restaurant has been in operation since 1956. A favourite haunt of actors and the literati, it has deep red walls lined with black and white images of the notables who have passed through its doors. Traditional classics include rack of lamb, steak, Dublin Bay prawns and tempting desserts. The service is intimate and welcoming.

Bang Café

11 Merrion Row, Dublin 2 **Tel** *01 676 0898*   **Map** E5

This hip restaurant is the essence of stylish minimalism; a fact that is reflected in its cuisine, as well as in the decor of natural tones and dark wood furnishings. The contemporary fare includes great fish dishes, mouth-watering scallops and excellent bangers and mash. The service is highly professional.

Browne's Brasserie

22 St Stephen's Green, Dublin 2 **Tel** *01 638 3939*   **Map** D4

This award-winning restaurant of the stylish Browne's Hotel *(see p129)* takes pride in its wonderfully romantic atmosphere. Elegantly furnished with antiques, the dining room is warm and welcoming, with friendly waiting staff. Good international cooking is backed up by delicious desserts.

Diep le Shaker

55 Pembroke Lane, Dublin 2 **Tel** *01 661 1829*   **Map** E5

Superb food and efficient service await at this bright, cheery Asian diner. Try prawn red curry served in the shell of a baby coconut, or the popular spicy beef curry. The layout is open-plan, and you can eat on the balcony overlooking the lower floor. Excellent exotic cocktails can be enjoyed at the bar. Live jazz Tuesdays and Wednesdays.

FXB

Pembroke Street, Dublin 2 **Tel** *01 676 4606*

Map *E5*

This quality traditional steakhouse and seafood chain enjoys a long-standing reputation of excellence. Meat is supplied by reliable butchers in Offaly. Sip a bubbly champagne cocktails as you wait for your meaty order to arrive. The popularity of this restaurant has led to other branches being opened in Temple Bar and Christchurch.

La Cave

28 South Anne Street, Dublin 2 **Tel** *01 679 4409*

Map *D4*

Descend the stairs from street level into a tiny cavernous wine bar that is also a restaurant offering French food of a high standard, sometimes with a North African flavour. The owner, Margaret, is one of Ireland's leading wine experts and offers an impressively extensive wine list, sourced everywhere from France to Uruguay. The wine bar is open late.

L'Gueuleton

1 Fade Street, Dublin 2 **Tel** *01 675 3708*

Map *C4*

Come to this popular French bistro for everything from snail and Roquefort Pithivier to duck with sweetened chicory, all accompanied by smooth jazz music in the background. Although it is not possible to make reservations in advance, there is a bar area where you can wait for a table. AmEx and Diner cards not accepted.

Nico's

53 Dame Street, Dublin 2 **Tel** *01 677 3062*

Map *D3*

Traditional Italian fare from a restaurant that has maintained a quiet, dignified presence on the scene for more than 30 years. Plush red drapes set the tone for the decor and for the traditional menu. For dessert, try the Italian *cassata* with Galliano. A piano player performs Tuesday to Saturday evenings, and there is an excellent wine list.

Dobbins Wine Bistro

15 Stephen's Lane, Dublin 2 **Tel** *01 661 3321*

Map *F5*

Popular since 1978, this cheerful bistro has a warm and pleasing ambience, with red and white checkered tablecloths and the floor scattered with sawdust. Given the good and extensive wine list, Dobbins is a popular spot for a leisurely liquid lunch. Among the highlights on the menu are smoked fish cakes and prime sirloin of beef.

Il Posto

10 St Stephen's Green, Dublin 2 **Tel** *01 679 4769*

Map *D4*

Il Posto is an oasis of calm from the bustle of Stephen's Green. Although the atmosphere is relaxed, this restaurant offers very formal dining. The food is of the highest standard, a mix of traditional and contemporary Italian, coupled with excellent service. In summer, try to get one of the tables on the terrace, with views of St Stephen's Green.

Jaipur

41–46 South Great George's Street, Dublin 2 **Tel** *01 677 0999*

Map *C4*

Often acclaimed as the best Indian restaurant in the city, Jaipur offers high-quality, innovative dishes. The decor, stylish and with a contemporary feel, features warm, tasteful colours. The restaurant is superbly managed by a well-informed and charming staff. Vegetarians are well catered for. Branches have now opened in Malahide and Dalkey.

L'Ecrivain

109a Lower Baggot Street, Dublin 2 **Tel** *01 661 1919*

Map *F5*

One of the best restaurants in Dublin, L'Ecrivain combines classic formality with contemporary cool. Authentic French cuisine with an Irish flavour includes delicacies such as Galway Bay oysters and caviar. Seasonal game and seafood, as well as tasty desserts and cheeses, also figure prominently on the menu. The service is highly polished and efficient.

Peploe's Wine Bistro

16 St Stephen's Green, Dublin 2 **Tel** *01 676 3144*

Map *D4*

Located in the basement of a Georgian building, Peploe's is a glamorous, cosy and immensely popular restaurant. It is also always rushed, due to the consistently high-quality food available. It provides an extensive wine list – more than 30 varieties of wine are served by the glass. Book in advance.

Shanahan's on the Green

119 St Stephen's Street, Dublin 2 **Tel** *01 407 0939*

Map *D5*

The most succulent steaks in Dublin are found at this renowned steakhouse, set in an elegantly furnished Georgian house. Though steeply priced, the food is consistently of the highest quality. The portions are gargantuan, so it is wise to skip the starter if you hope to finish your main. Seafood, too, is available at this superbly managed establishment.

Thorntons

128 St Stephen's Green, Dublin 2 **Tel** *01 478 7008*

Map *D4*

Haute cuisine is on the menu at this Michelin-starred restaurant in the Fitzwilliam Hotel *(see p129)*. Its small dining room gives it a sense of privacy, while the cream and gold decor adds to the cosy, bright atmosphere. Chef Kevin Thornton offers signature dishes such as braised suckling pig, loin of venison or roast quail with brioche.

Unicorn

12B Merrion Court, Dublin 2 **Tel** *01 676 2182*

Map *E4*

Situated around the corner from St Stephen's Green, Unicorn has maintained an excellent standard since it first opened in 1938. Its casual atmosphere is unparalleled and enhanced by the friendly waiting staff. The Italian-Mediterranean food served here is utterly delicious, and the veal is particularly appetizing.

Key to Price Guide *see p138* **Key to Symbols** *see back cover flap*

SOUTHWEST DUBLIN

Govinda's

4 Aungier Street, Dublin 2 **Tel** *01 475 0309*

Map *C4*

Bright, cheerful and bustling with energy, Govinda's is run by Hare Krishnas and offers filling and tasty vegetarian fare, such as samosas, pizzas and moussaka, not to mention vegan options. For dessert, try the upside-down pineapple cake. Sinead O'Connor is a regular here. Another branch can be found at 33 Middle Abbey Street.

Gruel

68a Dame Street, Dublin 2 **Tel** *01 670 7119*

Map *C3*

This tiny, quirky café blends the rustic with the innovative in its light snacks, soups and hot specials. The "roast in a roll" is delicious and a firm favourite among the colourful patrons. Good pizzas and tasty sweet dishes make it an ideal spot for a quick bite at affordable prices. Eat in or take away.

Leo Burdock's

2 Werburgh Street, Dublin 8 **Tel** *01 454 0306*

Map *B4*

The patrons of Leo Burdock's, the oldest fish-and-chip takeaway in Dublin, include the ordinary folk of Dublin, as well as the stars. The chips are made from top-grade Irish potatoes, and there is a wide choice of fish, including smoked cod, haddock and lemon-sole goujon. Service is efficient. There is another branch on Liffey Street.

Queen of Tarts

4 Cork Hill, Dame Street, Dublin 2 **Tel** *01 670 7499*

Map *C3*

Opposite Dublin Castle and Dublin City Hall, this charming little café is cosy and welcoming. In addition to freshly prepared soups, sandwiches and hot savoury tarts, there is a dazzling array of mouth-watering desserts, including chocolate fudge cake, fruit tarts and home-made biscuits. The ideal spot for a quick and reasonably priced snack.

Brasil

17 Upper Stephen Street, Dublin 2 **Tel** *01 405 3854*

Map *C4*

Just off South George's Street, this lively Brazilian restaurant offers as much beef as you can handle. The great value buffet *(churrasco)* features all-you-can-eat starters, plus five kinds of meat. The wine list is not particularly extensive, but it includes some good Portuguese offerings. Caipirinha cocktails flow liberally.

Chez Max

1 Palace Street, Dublin 2 **Tel** *01 633 7215*

Map *C3*

This cosy French diner at the gates of Dublin Castle is so authentic that it is hard to get a seat on account of all the French clients who come here for lunch. There is a covered back garden and a little terrace out front for alfresco dining. The good, simple French cuisine is classic; the signature dish is *boeuf bourguignon*.

Eden

Meeting House Square, Temple Bar, Dublin 2 **Tel** *01 670 5372*

Map *C3*

Featuring an outside terrace on the square, this split-level restaurant is bright and modern in design, with cool blue tiled walls and an open kitchen. Eden is famed for its sirloin steaks, cleverly arranged fish dishes and imaginative use of seasonal vegetables. The early evening menu provides excellent value for money.

Elephant & Castle

18 Temple Bar, Dublin 2 **Tel** *01 679 3121*

Map *D3*

Very lively, this American-style brasserie in the heart of Temple Bar is invariably crowded. Have the mouth-watering chicken wings to start, and continue with the good omelettes, steaks, hamburgers and salads, all available at affordable prices. Weekend brunches are also popular. Telephone bookings are not accepted.

Lord Edward

23 Christchurch Place, Dublin 8 **Tel** *01 454 2420*

Map *B4*

The oldest seafood restaurant in the city, Lord Edward is located above a cosy and traditional pub that serves lunch downstairs. It has changed little over the years and maintains an authentic, old-fashioned feel. The long-established waiters are renowned for their charming service.

Mongolian Barbecue

7 Anglesea Street, Dublin 2 **Tel** *01 670 4154*

Map *D3*

Mix your own meat and spices, and bring the resulting patty to a shared, massive, hot metal plate to sizzle to your satisfaction. And go back for seconds, thirds and fourths. Veggies follow the same steps using tofu instead of meat – they also get a free starter of samosa or a spring roll. Excellent value, particularly for lunch. Good Sunday brunch.

Monty's of Kathmandu

28 Eustace Street, Dublin 2 **Tel** *01 670 4911*

Map *C3*

This friendly Nepalese restaurant serves tasty and interesting fish, chicken and lamb dishes at affordable prices. Vegetarians are also well catered for. Try the dumplings or the tandoori butter chicken in a deliciously creamy sauce. Upstairs is more cheerful than the basement dining room. The service is good and the atmosphere relaxed.

Saba
26–28 Clarendon Street, Dublin 2 **Tel** *01 679 2000*

€€€ — **Map** *D4*

This slick Thai/Vietnamese eatery is a cut above the norm. Chef Trakoolwattana has previously cooked for the Thai royal family. Herbs, vegetables and fruit arrive weekly from Bangkok, ensuring fresh authentic flavours. The extensive menu features hake and banana leaf, red curry sauce, and crispy whole sea bass. Good vegetarian selection, too.

Darwin's
16 Aungier Street, Dublin 2 **Tel** *01 475 7511*

€€€€ — **Map** *C4*

Specializing in steaks made from certified organic meat from the proprietor's own butcher shop, this is a carnivore's dream. The menu also includes crab cakes and duck spring rolls, not to mention some vegetarian options. Dishes are prepared using quality ingredients and presented with flair. Unpretentious ambience, with warm, friendly service.

Les Frères Jacques
74 Dame Street, Dublin 2 **Tel** *01 679 4555*

€€€€ — **Map** *C3*

This elegant restaurant is French in style, cuisine, atmosphere and service. Seafood and game feature prominently on the balanced seasonal menus. Try the grilled lobster fresh from the tank, or the roast lamb casserole with courgette, aubergine (eggplant) and thyme. Classic desserts are also on the menu. The good wine list favours French labels.

The Mermaid Café
69–70 Dame Street, Dublin 2 **Tel** *01 670 8236*

€€€€ — **Map** *C3*

A bright, contemporary restaurant with large windows and wooden furniture, The Mermaid Café is a firm favourite for weekend brunches. There is a certain American East Coast ambience about it, which is also evident in specialities such as New England crab cakes. The chef makes creative use of high quality Irish artisanal produce.

Fallon & Byrne
11–17 Exchequer Street, Dublin 2 **Tel** *01 472 1010*

€€€€€ — **Map** *D3*

A New York-style food hall combined with a French restaurant and a superlative wine cellar. There is also a food shop on the ground floor and a restaurant upstairs. The restaurant is open, spacious and bright, and serves particularly tasty breads. The wines are incredible, but beware – you can pay in excess of 1,000 euros a bottle here.

The Tea Room
The Clarence Hotel, 6–8 Wellington Quay, Dublin 2 **Tel** *01 407 0800*

€€€€€ — **Map** *C3*

The Clarence Hotel is owned by rock band U2. Come in by the Essex Street entrance, opposite the Project Theatre, and savour excellent cuisine served in a stylish dining room. High ceilings and large windows create a bright and airy atmosphere. The food is innovative and seasonal, and the lunch menu is particularly good value.

NORTH OF THE LIFFEY

The Cobalt Café
16 North Great George's Street, Dublin 1 **Tel** *01 873 0313*

€ — **Map** *D3*

This daytime café offers a range of home-made soups, sandwiches and cakes, as well as the delicious signature dish, Chicken Cobalt. The café doubles as a gallery exhibiting the works of up-and-coming Irish artists; as a result, it is a popular venue for art lovers.

Epicurean Food Hall
Lower Liffey Street, Dublin 1

€ — **Map** *D2*

This food hall comprises a number of outlets serving international light meals and snacks. There is a communal dining area in the centre, or you can take your food away and enjoy it on a seat on the boardwalk overlooking the Liffey. Itsabagel's snacks and Burdock's fish and chips are on offer, as well as Turkish, Italian and Mexican cuisines.

Kingfisher Grill
166 Parnell Street, Dublin 1 **Tel** *01 872 8732*

€ — **Map** *C2*

Modestly decorated but immaculately maintained, Kingfisher Grill is a no-frills diner. Prompt service and cheap prices make it a good spot for the simple dishes many of us long for. Potato wedges and prawn cocktail are two of the more popular starters. Finish your meal with jelly or ice cream.

Panem
Ha'penny Bridge House, 21 Lower Ormond Quay, Dublin 1 **Tel** *01 872 8510*

€ — **Map** *C3*

This tiny café and bakery offers Italian and French food, freshly prepared using only high quality ingredients. The menu includes delicious croissants and focaccia with savoury fillings, sweet brioches with chocolate, home-baked biscuits and good coffee. The mouth-watering hot chocolate is made from dark Belgian chocolate. Friendly staff.

Ali Lang
Parnell Street, Dublin 1 **Tel** *01 874 6766*

€€ — **Map** *D1*

This cheerful and buzzing Chinese/Korean eatery is one of many emerging along Parnell Street, the fledgling Chinatown of Dublin. The food is tasty, filling and fantastic value. A great option for a group of friends is the Korean barbecue, where you cook strips of lean, tasty meat on a hot dish in the centre of the pine table.

Key to Price Guide *see p138* **Key to Symbols** *see back cover flap*

Cactus Jacks

Millennium Walkway, Middle Abbey Street, Dublin 1 **Tel** *01 874 6198*

Map C3

A recent addition to the popular chain begun in Galway, this restaurant is modern and slick, with a low-lit setting. Cactus Jacks is one of few Mexican restaurants in Dublin that succeed by keeping food simple but tasty, with steak, fish and vegetarian dishes that are lighter versions of traditional Mexican recipes. Nice frozen margaritas, too.

D.One Restaurant

IFSC, North Wall Quay, Dublin 1 **Tel** *01 856 1622*

Map F2

Built at the very edge of the River Liffey, D.One Restaurant enjoys a great waterside location. It is decorated in a clean, contemporary style with large windows to make the best of its waterside views. Traditional dishes such as fish and chips are given a modern twist here. The early dinner is excellent value.

101 Talbot

100–102 Talbot Street, Dublin 2 **Tel** *01 874 5011*

Map E2

A Mediterranean approach is reflected in the decor as much as the cuisine at 101 Talbot, livening up the rather drab street on which it is located. The early-bird menu is good value and attracts many theatre-goers. Vegetarians are spoiled for choice at this restaurant, which will also do its utmost to meet any other dietary requirements.

Stillroom Restaurant

Old Jameson Distillery, Bow Street, Dublin 1 **Tel** *01 807 2248*

Map A2

This restaurant is part of the Old Jameson Distillery complex, which lies on the site of the original 18th-century distillery. At lunchtime the legal eagles from the nearby Courts swoop in here to savour the comfort food on offer. Traditional dishes include a daily roast, as well as delicious sandwiches and soups.

Nancy Hands

30–32 Parkgate Street, Dublin 8 **Tel** *01 677 01498*

Traditional Irish cuisine is on the menu at this restaurant next to Phoenix Park and the zoo. The open fireplace and wood and stone decor give an old-world atmosphere to this relatively new pub. The fare is of a good standard, a mix of traditional bar food, carvery and more international offerings. The chowder is particularly good.

Bar Italia

Quartier Bloom, Lower Ormond Quay, Dublin 1 **Tel** *01 874 1000*

Map C3

The popular Bar Italia, specializing in Italian fare, is always a hive of activity around lunchtime, when patrons stream in for freshly prepared antipasti, risottos, grilled vegetables or the pasta specials. Desserts are also an attraction, as is the excellent – and strong! – espresso.

Rhodes D7

Capel Building, Mary's Abbey, Dublin 7 **Tel** *01 804 4444*

Map C2

Celebrity chef Gary Rhodes's first Irish restaurant features his unique cuisine, which has already earned him five Michelin stars. On the walls is commissioned art by renowned Irish artist Deborah Donnelly. Try eel for starters, or a plate of three tomato soups. Finish your meal with Bailey's crème brûlée. No kids after 9pm.

Winding Stair

40 Lower Ormond Quay, Dublin 1 **Tel** *01 872 7320*

Map D3

At this slick and popular contemporary Irish restaurant, dishes include smoked haddock poached in milk with onions and white cheddar mash, or boiled Irish bacon collar with buttered new-season organic cabbage, mash and parsley sauce. Ingredients are organic and local where possible – even the chorizo is made in Ireland. No Diner or AmEx.

Chapter One

18–19 Parnell Square, Dublin 1 **Tel** *01 873 2266*

Map C1

In the centre of the Dublin Writers' Museum, Chapter One is often cited by critics as the best restaurant north of the Liffey. Relish the imaginative European cuisine, with an Irish twist, in a dining room of great character and comfort. The pre-theatre menu is a favourite among regulars who frequent the nearby Gate Theatre.

Ely chq

Stack A, Mayor Street, IFSC, Dublin 1 **Tel** *01 672 0010*

Map F2

This offshoot of the Ely Wine Bar *(see p139)* boasts a stylish and contemporary decor. The food – whether from the bar or à la carte menu – is fresh and tasty, and there is an exceptional wine list, with almost 100 wines by the glass. Eat alfresco on the covered terrace, in the cavernous basement or in the spacious, ground floor interior.

FURTHER AFIELD

Angler's Rest

Knockmaroon Hill, Strawberry Beds, Chapelizod, Dublin 20 **Tel** *01 820 4351*

Long known as a watering hole for fishermen along the river, the Angler's Rest has an open fire, timber ceilings and floors, and comfortable seating. Specials include seafood chowder and platter – fish is delivered daily from Howth. At weekends there is live music, featuring a mix of artists. Michael Collins used to be a regular in the Salmon Bar.

Aqua Restaurant

1 West Pier, Howth, Co Dublin **Tel** *01 832 0690*

This first floor restaurant, with lovely views over the sea and harbour, was formerly a yacht club, now converted into a bright contemporary space. The cuisine betrays a Californian-Italian influence; prominent on the menu are steaks, as well as fish and chicken dishes. The set menus are good value. Sunday brunch is accompanied by live jazz.

Independent Pizza

28 Lower Drumcondra Road, Dublin 7 **Tel** *01 830 2044*

This pizza house, owned by Gotham City crew *(see p139)*, serves delicious, surprising and light American-style pizza, said to be the best in Dublin. Try the Texas Chicken, the Thai Spice or the Pizza of the Month. A good wine list is also available. Book ahead if you can: the place is extremely popular and always busy.

Johnnie Fox's

Glencullen, Co Dublin **Tel** *01 295 5647*

About 30 minutes' drive south of the city, on the way up to the Dublin Mountains, this friendly pub has good Irish food, traditional music and dancing. Pan-seared scallops, crab salad, smoked salmon and sirloin steak are on the menu. The "Hooley Night", featuring dinner and a traditional show, attracts overseas visitors. Book ahead.

Beaufield Mews Restaurant, Gardens & Antiques

Woodlands Ave, Stillorgan, Co Dublin **Tel** *01 288 0375*

One of County Dublin's oldest restaurants, Beaufield Mews is beautifully set in an 18th-century cobbled courtyard with a rose garden to the rear. Good modern European food is served in an elegant dining room decorated with Irish art and antiques. An inviting atmosphere prevails throughout.

Bon Appetit

9 St James Terrace, Malahide, Co Dublin **Tel** *01 845 0314*

Situated in a renovated terrace near the marina, this well respected restaurant is inviting, with its warm colours, art collection and excellent seafood. Try the fresh prawn bisque with cognac, the Sole Creation McGuirk and the roast crispy duckling in Gran Marnier sauce. Desserts are equally tempting. Book in advance.

Dali's Restaurant

63–65 Main Street, Blackrock, Co Dublin **Tel** *01 278 0660*

At this chic, small restaurant with a distinctive contemporary feel, menus are appealingly light and colourful. Highlights include variations on classic themes, such as seared scallops and Dublin Bay prawns. The set lunch menus offer particularly good value for money. There is also a good wine list and a varied cheese selection.

Expresso Bar Café

1 St Mary's Road, Ballsbridge, Dublin 4 **Tel** *01 660 0585*

This restaurant is decorated in a contemporary, minimalist style. Open from breakfast, it is popular for lunch and weekend brunches. The traditional Irish fare, featuring chicken, fish, steaks and Irish beefburgers, uses high quality ingredients. The bread-and-butter pudding makes a perfect dessert. The service could be friendlier, though.

The Forty Foot

Pavilion Centre, Dun Laoghaire, Co Dublin **Tel** *01 284 2982*

After a walk on the pier, relax in this very modern upstairs restaurant and watch the day fade over Dublin Bay. The views are the main attraction at The Forty Foot, but the food is also appealing. Try the tian of crab and salmon with crème fraîche. Pleasant and competent staff.

Nosh

111 Coliemore Road, Dalkey, Co Dublin **Tel** *01 284 0666*

Nosh is contemporary in style, with light wood furniture. The well-balanced menus feature good fish and vegetarian dishes, as well as succulent steaks. Cod and chips, pea and asparagus risotto, and seared scallops also make appearances. The home-made desserts are good. The weekend brunch is very popular, as is the early-bird menu.

Abbey Tavern

Abbey Street, Howth, Co Dublin **Tel** *01 839 0307*

Open fires, linen-clad tables, fresh flowers and a slightly old-fashioned atmosphere define this restaurant on the first floor of a characteristic pub. Good, uncomplicated fish and meat dishes are served. The traditional Irish evening downstairs, featuring set dinners, is popular with visitors.

Brasserie Na Mara

1 Harbour Road, Dun Laoghaire, Co Dublin **Tel** *01 280 6767*

Conveniently located beside the harbour, ferry terminal and DART station, the welcoming Brasserie Na Mara is housed in a graceful period building. The stylish contemporary decor features large windows, linen-clad tables and fresh flowers. Seafood is a speciality, and the home-made desserts are delicious.

Caviston's Seafood Restaurant

59 Glasthule Road, Dun Laoghaire, Sandycove, Co Dublin **Tel** *01 280 9245*

Stunning seafood, prepared with simple flair, is on the menu at Caviston's. Sadly, this culinary cult address is only open for lunch, so be sure to book early and reserve the last sitting so that you can enjoy a leisurely afternoon lingering over coffee and dessert. The adjoining delicatessen sells delectable fare great for a picnic.

Key to Price Guide *see p138* **Key to Symbols** *see back cover flap*

King Sitric Fish Restaurant and Accommodation

East Pier, Howth, Co Dublin **Tel** *01 832 5235*

Named after the medieval Norse king of Dublin, this restaurant is acclaimed for good seafood and game. The dining room is stylishly modern, with scenic views. Specialities include crab bisque, Balscadden Bay lobster, black sole meunière and fillet steak with forest mushrooms. Excellent wine cellar.

The Lobster Pot

9 Ballsbridge Terrace, Ballsbridge, Dublin 4 **Tel** *01 660 9170*

This long-established upstairs restaurant deservedly commands a loyal following. High-quality food is well presented and served by professional, charming waiters. Specialities feature dressed Kilmore crab, Dublin Bay prawns in Provençal sauce, generously sized sole on the bone, delicious steaks, and chicken and game dishes.

The Queens

Castle Street, Dalkey **Tel** *01 285 4569*

Established in 1745, The Queens is one of Ireland's oldest hostelries, right in the centre of Dalkey. It has grown into an award-winning restaurant serving everything from hamburgers to steamed mussels, or bacon and cabbage. The most pleasant tables are those located out front, with a view of the battlements of Goat's Castle, next door.

Roly's Bistro

7 Ballsbridge Terrace, Ballsbridge, Dublin 4 **Tel** *01 668 2611*

In the heart of Ballsbridge, this lively, bustling bistro offers reliable, colourful and delicious food. Try the Kerry lamb pie or the Dublin Bay prawns Provençal. Other delicacies include fish and game dishes and succulent steaks. Sit upstairs, if possible, and take home the delicious home-made breads, which are for sale. Reservations are advised.

The Washerwoman's

62a Glasnevin Hill, Dublin 9 **Tel** *01 837 9199*

A short stroll from the Botanic Gardens, this cosy restaurant is housed in an 18th-century building, one of the oldest in Glasnevin. It serves traditional food made from locally sourced ingredients. Try the pork belly with cider sauce, and the delicious chocolate brownies. While you eat, enjoy the original artworks on the walls – they are all for sale.

Mint

47 Ranelagh Village, Dublin 6 **Tel** *01 497 8655*

This acclaimed French restaurant uses both rustic and luxurious ingredients to create food that looks like a work of art, as well as tasting divine. Try the lasagne of rabbit or the roasted John Dory. The meal usually comes with delicious little extras. An extensive wine list and a wide range of cheeses, mostly Irish, complete the picture.

BEYOND DUBLIN

O'Brien's Good Food and Drink House

The Village, Johnstown, Navan, Co Meath **Tel** *046 902 0555*

The menu at this award-winning gastropub with wood panelling, brick walls and a rustic feel includes spring rolls and pizzas. Seafood dishes are a speciality: try the Seafood Surprise, a pie dish full of prawns, salmon, monkfish and other sea creatures. Leave some room for the ginger and honeycomb pudding. Live music on Friday nights.

Franzini O'Brien's

French's Lane, by Trim Castle, Co Meath **Tel** *046 943 1002*

Modern and crisp in both decor and cuisine, this restaurant beside Trim Castle offers contemporary European cuisine. Food is prepared simply but to a high standard, and includes chicken and pasta dishes, pizzas and steaks. Vegetarians will have plenty of choice, too. The staff are very welcoming, and there is a good wine list.

The Harvest Room

Arthurstown, Co Wexford **Tel** *051 389 600*

TV chef Kevin Dundon, one of Ireland's best, runs a cookery school at this award-winning restaurant at the Dunbrody Country House Hotel. The understated dishes rely on the freshness and quality of locally sourced seasonal ingredients – some from the kitchen garden and orchard. The airy dining room overlooks the garden. No children after 8pm.

The Strawberry Tree

Brooklodge Hotel, Macreddin Village, Co Wicklow **Tel** *0402 36444*

Ireland's only certified organic restaurant, at the Brooklodge Hotel, serves only wild and organic foods sourced from local artisan suppliers. Large feasts can be arranged for parties of eight or more. Try the wild wood pigeon terrine with strawberry and green pepper jam, or the carrot and orange sorbet, described by critics as "a slice of heaven".

Wineport Lodge

Glasson, Athlone, Co Westmeath **Tel** *090 643 9010*

Ireland's first wine hotel is housed in a modern, cedar-clad structure on the shores of Lough Ree – you can even arrive by boat if you wish. The mission statement says they believe in good food, great wine and relaxation, and they certainly deliver on all three. Seasonal local food is creatively mastered. The wine list is extensive.

Pubs, Bars and Cafés

Dublin's pubs are a slice of living history, famous as the haunts of literary figures, politicans and rock stars alike. Today, as well as the memorabilia on the walls, it is the singing, dancing, talk and laughter that make a pub tour of Dublin a necessity *(see p156)*.

There are nearly 1,000 pubs inside the city limits. Some excel in entertainment, others in the quality of their Guinness and their pub food, but there are also many modern bars to match the best in Europe.

In recent years Dublin has become very cosmopolitan and, as well as the pubs, there is a wide range of cafés offering quick and inexpensive food. The ones listed here are good for those on a busy sightseeing schedule.

TRADITIONAL PUBS

Each Dublin pub has its own character and, while many of them are rather touristy, they retain a trade-mark clientèle: **Doheny & Nesbitt** and the **Horseshoe Bar** attract politicians, journal-ists and lawyers while **Neary's** pulls in a theatrical crowd. Others have a strong literary connection; Brendan Behan drank at **McDaid's** while **Davy Byrne's** was featured in Joyce's *Ulysses*. Some of the best and most ornate interiors include **The Brazen Head**, the **Stag's Head**, the **Long Hall** and **Kehoe's** with its great snugs. **Mulligan's**, founded in 1782, claims to have the best Guinness. If you fancy something different, **Porter House** in Parliament Street brews its own, including an excellent oyster stout.

MUSIC PUBS

Regular traditional music sessions take place all over Dublin. **The Brazen Head, O'Donoghue's** and the **Cobblestone** are popular venues. The **International Bar** focuses on singers and comedians, while **Whelan's** has a proper venue room next door with an eclectic range of acts for a cover charge of under 10 euros.

MODERN BARS

Recently, a number of Continental-style bars have cropped up which cater to a young and fashionable crowd. **Hogan's**, and the **Globe** are on the edge of Temple Bar. The main bar at the **Clarence Hotel** does great cocktails. Inventive drinks are also on the menu at the trendy **Chocolate Bar**. **Café en Seine** near Trinity College has a wide choice of food and offers a live jazz brunch on Sunday.

PUB FOOD

Many of Dublin's grand old pubs offer tasty and good-value pub lunches. Just off Grafton Street are **O'Neill's** and the very traditional **Old Stand**. In Temple Bar, **Oliver St John Gogarty** is probably the best option.

MUSEUM AND SHOP CAFES

Many of Dublin's tourist attractions offer good-quality cafés and snack bars. One of the best is at the **National Gallery**: it serves mainly Mediterranean food and is operated by the Fitzer's chain. Food at the **National Museum** has more of a tradi-tional Irish choice while the **Irish Film Institute** offers an eclectic range. Food at **Avoca** is modern and delicious: go early if you want to get in. For a unique place to eat, try the upstairs café at the **Winding Stair Bookshop**.

BREAKFAST

Most hotels and B&Bs in the city serve reasonable break-fasts, an essential start to a full day's sightseeing. A part-icular favourite of Dubliners is **Café Java**, while **Heavenly Café** serves great-value food and a nice variety of breakfasts. **Café Kylemore** also makes a good breakfast.

COFFEE AND CAKES

In an attractive setting among the stalls at Powerscourt Townhouse, **Mimo** offers coffee, fresh food and a good wine selection in a relaxed, spacious environment.

PIZZA AND PASTA

Irish-Italian cafés and restaurants offer some of the best-value meals in the city. Two very popular ones, the family-oriented **Little Caesar's Palace** and the tiny **Steps of Rome**, lie off Grafton Street, as does the excellent **Pasta Fresca**. Temple Bar's **Bad Ass Café** has a youthful feel and serves pizza, pasta and salads. Sinéad O'Connor worked here before making it in music. **Milano**, currently with two branches in the city, is a branch of the popular British chain Pizza Express.

TRADITIONAL FOOD

For traditional food with a modern slant, **Gallagher's Boxty House**, specialising in Irish pancakes, is a popular choice. However, some might prefer the even simpler fare at **Café Kylemore** which is run by a major city bakery. For good honest fish and chips try the venerable **Leo Burdock's**.

VEGETARIAN

One of the great favourites is the long-running café, **Cornucopia**, also open for breakfast and lunch. **Café Fresh** is a fun place to eat in the Powerscourt Townhouse while **Juice** offers a cool, modern feel. The **Alamo Café** is the pick of the city's Mexican restaurants and offers lots of choice for vegetarians but also serves meat dishes. Temple Bar's Saturday market has a good organic selection.

DIRECTORY

TRADITIONAL PUBS

The Brazen Head
20 Bridge St Lower.
Map A3.
Tel 679 5186.

Davy Byrne's
21 Duke St.
Map D4.
Tel 677 5217.

Doheny & Nesbitt
5 Lower Baggot St.
Map F5.
Tel 676 2945.

Horseshoe Bar
Shelbourne Hotel,
27 St Stephen's Green.
Map E4.
Tel 663 4500.

John Kehoe's
9 Anne St South.
Map D4.
Tel 677 8312.

The Long Hall
51 South Great George's
St. **Map** C4.
Tel 475 1590.

McDaid's
3 Harry St.
Map D4.
Tel 679 4395.

Mulligan's
8 Poolbeg St.
Map E3.
Tel 677 5582.

Neary's
1 Chatham St.
Map D4.
Tel 677 8596.

Porter House
16–18 Parliament St.
Map C3.
Tel 679 8847.

Stag's Head
1 Dame Court,
off Dame St. **Map** C3.
Tel 679 3687.

MUSIC BARS

Cobblestone
77 North King St.
Map A2.
Tel 872 1799

International Bar
23 Wicklow St.
Map D3.
Tel 677 9250.

O'Donoghue's
15 Merrion Row.
Map E5.
Tel 676 2807.

Whelan's
25 Wexford St.
Map C5.
Tel 478 0766.

MODERN BARS

The Café Bar
Morrison Hotel,
Ormond Quay.
Map C3.
Tel 887 2400.

Café en Seine
40 Dawson St.
Map D4.
Tel 677 4567.

Chocolate Bar
Harcourt St, at Hatch St
Lower. **Map** D5.
Tel 478 0166.

The Globe
11 South Great George's
St. **Map** C4.
Tel 671 1220.

Hogan's
35 South Great George's
St. **Map** C4.
Tel 677 5904.

Octagon Bar
Clarence Hotel,
6–8 Wellington Quay.
Map C3.
Tel 670 9000.

PUB FOOD

The Old Stand
37 Exchequer St.
Map D3.
Tel 677 7220.

Oliver St John Gogarty
57 Fleet St.
Map D3.
Tel 671 1822.

O'Neill's
2 Suffolk St.
Map D3.
Tel 679 3656.

MUSEUM AND SHOP CAFES

Avoca Café
11–13 Suffolk St.
Map D3.
Tel 286 7466.

Irish Film Institute
6 Eustace St,
Temple Bar.
Map C3.
Tel 679 3477.

National Gallery
Merrion Square West.
Map E4.
Tel 661 5133.

National Museum
Kildare St.
Map E4.
Tel 677 7444.

Winding Stair Bookshop
40 Ormond Quay Lower.
Map C3.
Tel 872 7320.

BREAKFAST

Café Java
145 Leeson St.
Map E5.
Tel 660 0675.

Heavenly Café
87 Lower Camden St.
Map C5.
Tel 405 3990.

COFFEE AND CAKES

Mimo
Powerscourt Townhouse,
South William St.
Map D4.
Tel 679 4160.

PIZZA AND PASTA

Bad Ass Café
9 Crown Alley,
Temple Bar.
Map D3.
Tel 671 2596.

Little Caesar's Palace
1–3 Balfe St. **Map** D4.
Tel 670 4534.

Milano
38 Dawson St.
Map D4.
Tel 670 7744.
19 Essex St East.
Map C3.
Tel 670 3384.

Pasta Fresca
4 Chatham St.
Map D4.
Tel 679 2402.

Steps of Rome
Unit 1, Chatham Court,
Chatham St.
Map D4.
Tel 670 5630.

TRADITIONAL FOOD

Café Kylemore
O'Connell St.
Map D2.
Tel 872 2138.

Gallagher's Boxty House
Temple Bar.
Map D3.
Tel 677 2762.

Leo Burdock's
2 Werburgh St.
Map C4.
Tel 454 0306.

VEGETARIAN

Alamo Café
22 Temple Bar.
Map C3.
Tel 677 6546.

Cafe Fresh
Powerscourt Townhouse,
South William St.
Map D4.
Tel 671 9669.

Cornucopia
19 Wicklow St.
Map D3.
Tel 677 7583.

Juice
9 Castlehouse
South Great George's St.
Map C4.
Tel 475 7856.

SHOPS AND MARKETS

Dublin is a paradise for shoppers, with its wide streets, indoor markets, craft stores and out-of-town shopping centres. Popular buys include chunky Aran sweaters, Waterford crystal, Irish linen, hand-loomed tweed from Donegal and tasty farmhouse cheeses. The thriving crafts industry is based on traditional products with an innovative twist. Typical of contemporary Irish crafts are good design, quality craftsmanship and a range spanning

Modern Irish pottery

Celtic brooches and bone china, knitwear and designer fashion, carved bogwood and books of Irish poetry. Kitsch souvenirs also abound, from leprechauns and shamrock emblems to Guinness tankards and garish religious memorabilia. Irish whiskeys and liqueurs are always popular and very reasonable to buy in Dublin.

In the directory on page 151, a map reference is given for each address that features on the Dublin Street Finder map on pages 180–81.

Johnson's Court alley behind Grafton Street in southwest Dublin

WHERE TO SHOP

There are two major shopping quarters in Dublin. The north side of the Liffey, centred on O'Connell and Henry streets, has several shopping centres and department stores. The famous Moore Street fruit and vegetable market is held Monday to Saturday just off Grafton Street. More upmarket shops can be found on the south side, around Grafton and Nassau streets. The Temple Bar area contains a number of trendy craft shops.

WHEN TO SHOP

Most shops are open from Monday to Saturday, 9am to 5:30 or 6pm. Shops open late on Thursday nights. Shops are closed at Easter and Christmas and on St Patrick's Day but are open on most other public holidays.

HOW TO PAY

Major credit cards such as VISA and MasterCard are accepted in most large stores, but smaller shops may prefer cash. Traveller's cheques are accepted in major stores with a passport as identification. Eurocheques are generally no longer acceptable.

SALES TAX AND REFUNDS

Most purchases are subject to VAT (sales tax) at 21 per cent, a sum included in the sales price. However, visitors from outside the European Union (EU) can reclaim VAT prior to departure. If you are shipping goods overseas, refunds can be claimed at the point of purchase. If taking your goods with you, look for the CashBack logo in shops, fill in the special voucher, then visit the CashBack offices at Dublin airport.

SHOPPING CENTRES

Dublin has several large shopping centres, including the **Dundrum Shopping Centre**, voted the best in Europe in 2007. The **Dun Laoghaire Shopping Centre** is on several floors and has a huge range of clothes shops, bookshops and electronics shops. In central Dublin are the **St Stephen's Green Shopping Centre** and the **Jervis Shopping Centre**, both offering the comfort of covered shopping. A more unusual centre is the **Powerscourt Townhouse** *(see p60)*, more of an indoor market than a shopping centre, selling various Irish crafts.

BOOKS

Bookshops abound in Dublin. **Eason and Son**, on O'Connell Street, is the biggest bookseller in the city with a wide range of Irish literature and national and

The Ha'penny Bridge Galleries on Bachelors Walk

Brown Thomas department store on Grafton Street

international newspapers. For antiquarian books, **Cathach Books** on Duke Street has an excellent selection.

Foreign-language books are available in Dublin – try **International Books** for the best range. **Hodges Figgis** specializes in Irish literature and academic publications. They also have a coffee shop in the store. One of the best for general books is the **Dublin Bookshop** on Grafton Street (part of the Dubray Books chain). On two floors, they have an extensive Irish section and a good range of tourist guides as well as general fiction and children's books. **Waterstone's** and **Hughes & Hughes** are also both good general booksellers.

MUSIC

Traditional musical instruments are made in many regions of Ireland, but Dublin has a history of specializing in hand-made harps. Several shops sell musical instruments, such as hand-crafted bodhráns (traditional goatskin hand-held drums) and uilleann pipes (bagpipes). **Waltons** sells traditional instruments and sheet music, while **Claddagh Records** is a specialist folk shop, selling Irish folk and ethnic music. For a standard range of pop and classical music there are two branches of the **HMV** music store in Dublin.

ANTIQUES

Dublin has its own antiques centre, in the form of Francis Street in the south west of the city. **Lantern Antiques** specializes in old pub fittings such as mirrors and old advertisements. For rugs and carpets try **Forsyth Antiques**. For 20th-century decorative arts visit **Johnston Antiques. The Ha'penny Bridge Galleries** sell everything from furniture through to cast iron and marble. **Courtville Antiques** in the Powerscourt Townhouse has a beautiful collection of antique jewellery, silver, paintings and objets d'art. On Grafton Street, **McCormack** is particularly good for antique jewellery.

Sign outside Eason and Son

CRAFTS

Whichcraft at the Designyard Gallery in Cow's Lane and the **Irish Celtic Craftshop** in Lord Edward Street have a great

Bodhráns of perfect pitch for sale in Dublin

range of contemporary Irish crafts. The Crafts Council also recommends other good outlets for Irish crafts, and the tourist offices have lists of local workshops, where you can often watch the production process. **The Kilkenny Shop** sells tiles, rugs, metal-, leather- and woodwork.

JEWELLERY

In its golden age, Celtic metalwork was the pride of Ireland. Many contemporary craftspeople are still inspired by traditional designs on Celtic chalices and ornaments. Silver and gold jewellery is made all over Ireland in many designs and widely available in Dublin. The Claddagh ring is the most famous of all – the lovers' symbol of two hands cradling a heart with a crown. In the Powerscourt Townhouse, shops have handmade and antique jewellery on display and gold- and silversmiths can be seen at work. **McDowell** jewellers specialize in handcrafted gold and silver Irish jewellery.

CHINA, CRYSTAL AND GLASSWARE

Ireland's most famous make of crystalware is Waterford Crystal. Still made today in the town of Waterford, south of Dublin, this beautiful crystal and glassware is known all over the world for its outstanding quality.

Dublin Crystal, in Blackrock, south of the city, makes and sells on the premises fine-quality hand-cut crystal.

There are many producers of fine china in Ireland. Royal Tara China in Galway is Ireland's leading fine bone china manufacturer, with designs incorporating Celtic themes. The best place to buy china and glassware is in department stores, such as Clery's and Brown Thomas.

LINEN

Damask linen was brought to Armagh in Northern Ireland by Huguenot refugees fleeing French persecution. Linen is widely available all over Ireland today, and fine Irish linen can be bought at many outlets in Dublin, including the **Brown Thomas** department store, which has an excellent linen shop. Another good supplier is **Murphy, Sheehy and Co**, who are located behind the Powerscourt Townhouse. As well as being famous for fine-quality Irish linen, they also sell tweeds.

Sign for the linen department at Brown Thomas store

KNITWEAR AND TWEED

Aran sweaters are sold all over Ireland, but originate in County Galway and the Aran Islands themselves, off the west coast of Ireland. One of Dublin's best buys, these oiled, off-white sweaters used to be handed down through generations of Aran fishermen. Legend has it that each family used its own motifs so that, if a fisherman were lost at sea and his body unidentifiable, his family could recognize him by his sweater. Warm and rain-resistant clothes are generally of good quality, from waxed jackets and duffel coats to sheepskin jackets. **House of Ireland** offer an excellent selection of quality Irish clothing. Knitwear is sold everywhere in Dublin.

Good buys include embroidered waistcoats and handwoven scarves. **The Sweater Shop** has woollens and tweeds at reasonable prices. The Suffolk Street branch of **Avoca** has a good mix of traditional and trendy.

Donegal tweed is noted for its texture and subtle colours (originally produced by local plant and mineral dyes). Tweed caps, scarves, ties, jackets and suits are sold in outlets such as **Kevin & Howlin** in Dublin. For menswear specialists, try **Kennedy & McSharry**.

FASHION

Inspired by a predominantly young population, Ireland is fast acquiring a name for fashion. Conservatively cut tweed and linen suits continue to be models of classic good taste, while younger designers are increasingly experimental, using bold lines and mixing traditional fabrics.

A-Wear is an Irish chain store that has a branch in Dublin. In the Design Centre in Powerscourt Townhouse Shopping Centre are clothes by the best Irish designers including John Rocha, Paul Costelloe, Louise Kennedy, Quin and Donnelly and Mariad Whisker. The department stores **Brown Thomas** and **Clery's** have an excellent selection of men's, women's and children's clothing. Shoe and clothing sizes are identical to British fittings.

Fresh cheeses in Meetinghouse Square

FOOD AND DRINK

Smoked salmon, home-cured bacon, farmhouse cheeses, preserves, soda bread and handmade chocolates make perfect last-minute gifts. **Butlers Chocolate Café**, sells particularly delicious handmade Irish chocolates. Several shops will package and send Irish salmon overseas.

Bewley's teas and coffees are sold in supermarkets like Tescos, **Dunnes** and Super Value all over Ireland. Guinness travels less well and is best drunk in Ireland. Irish whiskey is hard to beat as a gift or souvenir. Apart from the cheaper Power and Paddy brands, the big names are Bushmills and Jameson. Irish liqueurs to enjoy include Irish Mist and Bailey's Irish Cream.

Fresh fruit stall off O'Connell Street

DIRECTORY

SHOPPING CENTRES

Dundrum Shopping Centre
Sandyford Rd, Dundrum, Dublin 16.
Tel 299 1700.

Dun Laoghaire Shopping Centre
Marine Rd, Dun Laoghaire.
Tel 280 2981.

Jervis Shopping Centre
125 Abbey St Upper.
Map C2.
Tel 878 1323.

Powerscourt Townhouse Shopping Centre
South William St.
Map D4.
Tel 671 7000.

St Stephen's Green Shopping Centre
St Stephen's Green West.
Map D4.
Tel 478 0888.

BOOKS

Cathach Books
10 Duke St.
Map D4.
Tel 671 8676.
www.rarebooks.ie

Dublin Bookshop
36 Grafton St.
Map D4.
Tel 677 5568.

Eason and Son
80 Middle Abbey St.
Map D2.
Tel 858 3881.
www.eason.ie

Hodges Figgis
56–58 Dawson St.
Map D4.
Tel 677 4754.

Hughes & Hughes
St Stephen's Green Shopping Centre.
Map D4.
Tel 478 3060.
Also at
Dublin Airport.
Tel 704 4034.

International Books
18 Frederick St South.
Map E4.
Tel 679 9375.
www.international books.ie

Waterstone's
7 Dawson St.
Map D4.
Tel 679 1415.
Also at
Jervis Shopping Centre.
Map C2.
Tel 878 1311.
www.waterstones.co.uk

MUSIC

Claddagh Records
2 Cecilia St, Temple Bar.
Map C3.
Tel 677 0262.

HMV
18 Henry St.
Map D2.
Tel 873 2899.
Also at
Grafton St.
Map D4.
Tel 679 5334.

Waltons
3–5 Frederick St North.
Map C1.
Tel 874 7805.

JEWELLERY

McDowell
3 Upper O'Connell St.
Map D2.
Tel 874 4961.

ANTIQUES

Courtville Antiques
Powerscourt Townhouse Shopping Centre.
Map D4.
Tel 679 4042.

Forsyth Antiques
108 Francis St.
Map B4.
Tel 473 2148.

The Ha'penny Bridge Galleries
15 Bachelors Walk.
Map D3.
Tel 872 3950.

Johnston Antiques
69–70 Francis St.
Map B4.
Tel 473 2384.
www.johnston antiques.net

Lantern Antiques
56 Francis St.
Map B4.
Tel 453 4593.

McCormack
51 Grafton St.
Map D4.
Tel 677 3737.

CRAFTS

The Irish Celtic Craftshop
10–12 Lord Edward St.
Map C3.
Tel 679 9912.

The Kilkenny Shop
6 Nassau St.
Map E4.
Tel 677 7066.
www.kilkenny group.com

Whichcraft
Designyard Gallery, Cow's Lane, Temple Bar.
Map C3.
Tel 474 1011.
www.whichcraft.com

CERAMICS, CHINA AND CRYSTAL

Dublin Crystal
Dundrum Shopping Centre.
Tel 298 7302.
www.dublincrystal.com

LINENS

Brown Thomas Linen Department
Grafton St.
Map D4.
Tel 605 6666.

Murphy, Sheehy and Co
14 Castle Market.
Map D4.
Tel 677 0316.
www.murphysheehy fabrics.com

KNITWEAR AND TWEED

Avoca
11-13 Suffolk St.
Map D3.
Tel 677 4215.
www.avoca.ie

House of Ireland
37–38 Nassau St.
Map D4.
Tel 671 1111.
www.houseof ireland.com

Kennedy and McSharry
39 Nassau St.
Map D3.
Tel 677 8770.

Kevin and Howlin
31 Nassau St.
Map D3.
Tel 677 0257.

The Sweater Shop
9 Wicklow St.
Map D3.
Tel 671 3270.
www.sweatershop.ie

FASHION

A-Wear
26 Grafton St.
Map D4.
Tel 671 7200.
www.awear.ie

Brown Thomas
88–95 Grafton St.
Map D4.
Tel 605 6666.

Clery's
18–27 O'Connell St Lower.
Map D2.
Tel 878 6000.
www.clerys.ie

FOOD AND DRINK

Butlers Chocolate Café
51a Grafton St.
Map D4.
Tel 671 0599.

Dunnes
Henry St.
Map D2.
Tel 671 4629.

What to Buy in Dublin

St Brigid's cross

The many gift and craft shops scattered throughout Dublin make it easy to find Irish specialities to suit all budgets. The best buys include linen, tweeds and lead crystal. Local crafts make unique souvenirs, from delicate handmade silver jewellery and hand-thrown ceramics to traditional musical instruments. Religious artifacts are also widely available. Irish food and drink, especially whiskey, are evocative reminders of your trip.

Traditional hand-held drum
(*bodhrán*) and beater

Connemara marble
"worry stone"

Traditional
Claddagh ring

Modern jewellery and metalwork *draw on a long and varied tradition. Craftspeople continue to base their designs on sources such as the* Book of Kells *(see p40) and Celtic myths. Local plants and wildlife are also an inspiration. Claddagh rings – traditional betrothal rings – originated in County Galway but are widely available in Dublin.*

Enamel brooch

Fuchsia earring
from Dingle

Celtic design
enamel brooch

Celtic design
silver pendant

Donegal tweed jacket and waistcoat

Tweed jacket and skirt

Clothing *made in Ireland is usually of excellent quality. Tweed-making still flourishes in Donegal where tweed can be bought ready-made as clothing or hats or as lengths of cloth. Knitwear is widely available throughout Dublin in department stores and local craft shops. The many hand-knitted items on sale, including Aran jumpers, are not cheap but should give years of wear.*

Tweed cap

Tweed fisherman's hat

Aran jumper

Irish linen *is world-famous and the range unparalleled. There is a huge choice of table and bed linen, including extravagant bedspreads and crisp, formal tablecloths. On a smaller scale, tiny, intricately embroidered hand-kerchiefs make lovely gifts as do linen table napkins. Tea towels printed with colourful designs are widely available. You can also buy linen goods trimmed with fine lace, which is still hand-made in many parts of the country.*

Set of linen placemats and napkins

Fine linen handkerchiefs

Nicholas
Mosse
plate

Belleek
teapot

Nicholas
Mosse
cup

Irish ceramics *come in traditional and modern designs. You can buy anything from a full dinner service by established factories, such as Royal Tara China or the Belleek Pottery, to a one-off contemporary piece from a local potter's studio.*

·IRISH·
PROVERBS

ILLUSTRATED BY
KAREN BAILEY

Book of Irish Proverbs

Books and stationery *are often beautifully illustrated. Museums and bookshops stock a wide range.*

Irish crystal, *hand-blown and hand-cut, can be ordered or bought in many shops in Dublin. Pieces from the principal manufacturers, such as Waterford Crystal, Tyrone Crystal and Jerpoint Glass, from glasses and decanters to elaborate chandeliers, are widely sold.*

**Celtic design
cards**

**Waterford crystal tumbler
and decanter**

Food and drink *will keep the distinctive tastes of Dublin fresh long after you arrive home. Whiskey connoisseurs should visit the Old Jameson Distillery (see p75) to sample their choice of whiskeys. The Guinness Storehouse (see p82) is a must for aficionados of the dark stout. Good regional food can be found all over the Dublin area.*

| Jameson whiskey | Bushmills whiskey | Fruit cake made with Guinness | Jar of Irish marmalade | Packet of dried seaweed |

ENTERTAINMENT IN DUBLIN

Although Dublin is well served by theatres, cinemas, night-clubs and rock venues, what sets the city apart from other European capitals is its pubs. Lively banter, impromptu music sessions and great Guinness are the essential ingredients for an enjoyable night in any one of dozens of lively, atmospheric hostelries in Dublin.

One of the most popular entertainment districts is the Temple Bar area. Along this narrow network of cobbled streets you can find

Traditional Irish dancer

everything from traditional music in grand old pubs to the latest dance tracks in a post-industrial setting. The variety of venues makes the centre south of the Liffey the place to be at night, although the north side does boast the two most illustrious theatres, the largest cinemas and the 7,000-seater Point Theatre, a converted 19th-century rail terminal beside the docks. It is now the venue for all major rock concerts and stage musicals as well as some classical music performances.

The listings magazine *In Dublin*, published every other week

ENTERTAINMENT LISTINGS

The fortnightly listings magazine *In Dublin* is available from all newsagents. *Hot Press*, a national bimonthly newspaper that covers rock and traditional music, has comprehensive listings for Dublin. The *Dublin Event Guide* is a free sheet available from pubs, cafés, restaurants and record shops. Published every two weeks, it is particularly strong on the city's music and nightclub scene.

BOOKING TICKETS

Tickets for many events are available on the night, but it is safer to book in advance. The main venues accept payment over the telephone by all major credit cards. **Ticketmaster** accepts phone bookings by credit card for many of the major shows in and around Dublin, while **HMV** and **Dublin Tourism** (Suffolk Street) sell tickets for theatres and gigs.

NIGHTCLUBS

Dublin's clublife offers plenty of choice. **POD** (Place of Dance) and **Lillie's Bordello** are magnets for celebrities, models and visiting stars. The more laid-back **Rí-Rá** (Gaelic for "uproar") is at the cutting edge of R&B and dance music.

For a lounge atmosphere, head for **The Sugar Club** which offers live music and cocktails. **The River Club** is theoretically open to members only, but dress smart and you should be able to get in.

Renards is a hip three-tiered bar/nightclub attracting music and film stars. **Club M**, in the basement of Bloom's Hotel, plays chart, dance and R&B hits. Another popular basement club is **Boomerang**, with three bars, a state-of-the-art

Street entertainer in central Dublin

The decadent interior of Lillie's Bordello, reminiscent of a boudoir

sound system and a different music mix each night.

Nightclubs in Dublin are being replaced by "super pubs" with dance floors. This has led to the rise of the "club night", which hosts a particular DJ or music genre on a given night of the week. Check out the club nights at **POD**, named Crawdaddy and Tripod, which involve a mix of electro, break beats, house and hip hop.

On Friday and Saturday nights, the **Gaiety Theatre** turns into a club; the music varies from soul, Motown and R&B to indie and 80s hits. At **The Village**, DJs take to the decks every night, and there is karaoke on Sundays. The music at **The Hub** covers everything

Buskers playing on Grafton Street in Southeast Dublin

from retro grooves to contemporary house.

Spirit consists of three floors under the themes of Mind, Body and Soul and includes a holistic centre, as well as a club and bars. Fridays at **The Vaults** see a mix of electro house, progressive and techno trance, while Saturdays host R&B, hip hop, soul and funk.

The George, a gay pub and club that has been running since 1985, stages popular drag shows, as well as Irish and international acts.

Wax hosts blues, house and garage tracks, as well as a popular electro-house club night on Thursdays. Friday's Sub Zero is a mix of indie, ska, alternative and funk downstairs in **Thomas Read's** pub.

CLASSICAL MUSIC, OPERA AND DANCE

Dublin has a great venue in the **National Concert Hall**, a 19th-century exhibition hall that was redesigned and acoustically adapted in the 1980s. It is where the National Symphony Orchestra plays most Friday evenings. The programme also includes jazz, dance, opera, chamber music and some traditional music.

The **Hugh Lane Municipal Gallery of Modern Art** *(see p73)* has regular Sunday lunchtime concerts. Other classical venues include the **Royal Hospital Kilmainham** *(see p84)* and the **Royal Dublin Society (RDS)**. International opera is staged at the **Point Theatre**. The DGOS (Dublin Grand Opera Society) performs every April and November at the Gaiety Theatre on King Street South.

COMEDY

Murphy's Laughter Lounge is one of Dublin's top comedy venues, attracting big names from the world of stand-up comedy. Other venues include the **Olympia Theatre** for international stars and **The Ha'penny Bridge Inn**, Tuesday to Thursday, for local talent.

Murphy's Laughter Lounge

TRADITIONAL MUSIC AND DANCE

To many Irish people, the standard of music in a pub is just as important as the quality of the Guinness. Central Dublin has a host of pubs reverberating to the sound of bodhráns, fiddles and uilleann pipes. One of the most famous is **O'Donoghue's**, where the legendary Dubliners started out in the early 1960s. The long-established **Auld Dubliner** and **Cobblestone** are also renowned venues for local and foreign bands. **The Merry Ploughboy** hosts traditional nights with an exciting mix of music and dancing involving many of Ireland's finest talents. **The Farmhouse Bar** and the **Castle Inn** stage Irish cabaret featuring dancing, singing and lively, toe-tapping music.

ROCK, JAZZ, BLUES AND COUNTRY

Dublin has had a thriving rock scene ever since local band Thin Lizzy made it big in the early 1970s. U2's success acted as a further catalyst for local bands, and there is a gig somewhere in the city on most nights. **Whelan's** features the best new Irish bands nightly; the **International Bar** caters mostly for acoustic acts and singer-songwriters; and the **Ha'penny Bridge Inn** *(see Comedy)* has folk and blues on Fridays and Saturdays. Big names play at either the Point Theatre or, in summer, local sports stadia. **Slane Castle** hosts a big rock event every summer.

The **Temple Bar Music Centre** and **The Sugar Club** *(see Nightclubs)* offer jazz, blues, salsa, swing and latin throughout the year, with the **Heineken Green Energy Festival** in May. Country music also has a big following.

Crowds dancing at The Sugar Club

The glamorous Horseshoe Bar in the Shelbourne Hotel

HOTEL BARS

In recent years, the pubs of Dublin have become so popular, they have started to overflow. As a consequence, a new breed of bar has successfully taken off. The hotel bars are the city's sophisticated watering holes, appealing to those who wish to escape the raucous "craic" of the more traditional pubs.

The **Inn on the Green**, located in the Fitzwilliam Hotel, features Nineties cool metal decor. At the Merrion Hotel, you can hide from the hubbub of the city in the **Cellar Bar**. Trendy media types hang out at the mellow **Octagon Bar** at The Clarence Hotel, or at the **Lobo Bar** at the Morrison. However, if it is undiluted glamour you seek, head for a shot of whiskey in **The Horseshoe Bar**, located within the renowned Shelbourne Hotel.

PUB CRAWLS AND TOURS

There are a number of organized pub crawls in Dublin, most of which cover the character pubs and those with a long and colourful history. The **Dublin Literary Pub Crawl**, which starts in The Duke pub on Duke Street, is perhaps the most famous of these. The two-and-a-half-hour tours feature pubs once frequented by Ireland's most famous authors and playwrights.

Viking Splash Tours operate a land-and-water sightseeing tour of Dublin. This tour is carried out in an amphibious military vehicle decorated as a Viking ship and complete with Viking costumed driver.

A handful of tours around the city offer an insight into Dublin's dark and spooky history. **The Walk Macabre**, for example, visits scenes of murder and intrigue in the city. If you prefer to be driven around, the **Dublin Ghost Bus Tour** offers on-board entertainment as well as lessons in bodysnatching and the story behind Bram Stoker's *Dracula*.

If tracing Dublin's musical heritage is of more interest to you, join the **Music Hall of Fame**. This takes you to the sites where bands such as U2 and Thin Lizzy first found fame. The **Musical Pub Crawl** is another tour that traces the history of Irish music, with musicians performing from pub to pub.

The **Historical Walking Tour** of Dublin takes in many of the significant locations of the city's colourful past.

Record shop and ticket office in Crown Alley, Temple Bar

CINEMA

Dublin's cinemas have had a boost thanks to the success of Dublin-based films such as *My Left Foot* (1989), *The Commitments* (1991) and *Michael Collins* (1996) and a subsequent growth in the country's movie production industry.

The **Irish Film Institute** *(see p58)* opened its doors in 1992 and was a most welcome addition to the city's entertainment scene. Housed in an original 17th-century building in Temple Bar, the centre shows mostly independent and foreign films, along with a programme of lectures, seminars and masterclasses. It boasts two screens, a bar, a restaurant and an archive of old film material.

Another cinema whose repertoire is mostly art house is the **Screen**, near Trinity College. The large first-run cinemas, such as the **Savoy** and the multiplex **Cineworld**, are all located on the north side of the river. These usually offer reduced prices for their afternoon screenings and show late-night movies at the weekend.

Temple Bar's summer-long **Diversions** festival offers regular outdoor screenings of Irish and international films at Meeting House Square. Tickets are free and available from Temple Bar Properties.

"Mr Screen" cinema sign

One of the amphibious vehicles used by Viking Splash Tours

DIRECTORY

BOOKING TICKETS

HMV
18 Henry St. **Map** D2.
Tel 872 2095.
65 Grafton St. **Map** D4.
Tel 679 5334.

Ticketmaster
www.ticketmaster.ie

NIGHTCLUBS

Boomerang
Fleet Street. **Map** D3.
Tel 677 3333. www.
boomerangniteclub.com

Club M
Bloom's Hotel, Cope St.
Map D3. *Tel 671 5622.*
www.clubm.ie

Gaiety Theatre
South King St. **Map** D4.
Tel 677 1717.
www.gaietytheatre.ie

The George
South Great George's St.
Map C3. *Tel 478 2983.*

The Hub
23–24 Eustace St.
Map C3. *Tel 670 7655.*

Lillie's Bordello
Adam Court, off Grafton
St. **Map** D4. *Tel 679 9204.*

POD
Old Harcourt St train
station, Harcourt St.
Map D5. *Tel 478 0225.*
www.pod.ie

Renards
South Frederick St.
Map E4. *Tel 677 5876.*
www.renards.ie

Rí-Rá
11 South Great George's
St. **Map** C3. *Tel 671 1220.*

The River Club
Merchants' Arch. **Map** D3.
Tel 677 2382.

Spirit
57 Middle Abbey St.
Map D2. *Tel 877 9999.*
www.spiritdublin.com

The Sugar Club
8 Lower Leeson St.
Map E5. *Tel 678 7188.*

Thomas Reads
Parliament Street.
Map C3.
Tel 677 1487.

The Vaults
Harbourmaster Place.
Map F2. *Tel 605 4700.*
www.thevaults.ie

The Village
26 Wexford St. **Map** C5.
Tel 475 8555.
www.thevillagevenue.com

Wax
Powerscourt Townhouse
Ctr, South William St.
Map D4. *Tel 677 0014.*
www.spydublin.com
www.electricity-
dublin.com

CLASSICAL MUSIC, OPERA AND DANCE

Hugh Lane Municipal Gallery of Modern Art
Charlemont House,
Parnell Sq North. **Map** C1.
Tel 222 5550.
www.hughlane.ie.

National Concert Hall
Earlsfort Terrace. **Map** D5.
Tel 417 0077.
www.nch.ie

Point Theatre
East Link Bridge,
North Wall Quay. **Map** F2.
Tel 836 6777.
www.thepoint.ie

Royal Dublin Society (RDS)
Ballsbridge. **Tel** 668 0866.
www.rds.ie

Royal Hospital Kilmainham
Kilmainham, Dublin 8.
Tel 612 9900.
www.modernart.ie

COMEDY

The Ha'penny Bridge Inn
Wellington Quay.
Map C3. *Tel 677 0616.*

Murphy's Laughter Lounge
4–6 Eden Quay. **Map** D2.
Tel 874 4611.

Olympia Theatre
Dame St. **Map** C3.
Tel 679 3323.

TRADITIONAL MUSIC & DANCE

Auld Dubliner
24–25 Temple Bar.
Map D3. *Tel 677 0527.*

Castle Inn
5–7 Lord Edward St.
Map C3. *Tel 475 1122.*

Cobblestone
77 King St North.
Map A2. *Tel 872 1799.*

The Farmhouse Bar
Rathfarnham, Dublin 16.
Tel 494 2311.

The Merry Ploughboy
Rockbrook, Rathfarnham,
Dublin 16.
Tel 493 1495.

O'Donoghue's
15 Merrion Row.
Map E5. *Tel 676 2807.*

ROCK, JAZZ, BLUES, SALSA AND COUNTRY

Heineken Green Energy Festival
Tel 284 1747.
www.mcd.ie

International Bar
23 Wicklow St.
Map D3.
Tel 677 9250.

Slane Annual Rock Concert
Slane Castle, Co Meath
Tel 041 988 4400.
www.slanecastle.ie

Temple Bar Music Centre
Curved St, Temple Bar.
Map E4.
Tel 670 9202.
www.tbmc.ie

Whelan's
25 Wexford St.
Map C5.
Tel 478 0766.
www.whelanslive.com

HOTEL BARS

Cellar Bar
Merrion Hotel,
24 Merrion St Upper.
Map E5.
Tel 603 0600.

The Horseshoe Bar
Shelbourne Hotel, 27 St
Stephen's Green North.
Map E4. *Tel 663 4500.*

Inn on the Green
Fitzwilliam Hotel, 12 St
Stephen's Green West.
Map D4. *Tel 478 7000.*

The Lobo Bar
The Morrison,
Ormond Quay. **Map** C3.
Tel 878 2999.

Octagon Bar
The Clarence,
6–8 Wellington Quay.
Map C3. *Tel 407 0800.*

PUB CRAWLS AND TOURS

Dublin Bus Ghost Tour
Tel 873 4222.

Dublin Literary Pub Crawl
Tel 670 5602.

Historical Walking Tour
Tel 878 0227.

Musical Pub Crawl
Tel 475 3313.

Music Hall of Fame
Tel 878 3345.

Viking Splash Tours
Tel 707 6000.

The Walk Macabre
Tel 087 677 1512.

CINEMA

Cineworld
Parnell Centre, Parnell St.
Map C2. *Tel 1520 880
444.* www.cineworld.ie

Diversions
Meeting House Square.
Map C3. *Tel 677 2255.*
www.templebar.ie

Irish Film Institute
6 Eustace St. **Map** C3.
Tel 679 5744. www.ifi.ie

Savoy
O'Connell St. **Map** D2.
Tel 874 8487.
www.savoy.ie

Screen
D'Olier St. **Map** D3.
Tel 672 5500.
www.screencinema.ie

Theatre in Dublin

Dublin is synonymous with theatre, having produced some of the greatest practitioners of the art in both English and Gaelic. It is not surprising, therefore, that with the economic boom of the 1990s, theatre was one of the areas to flourish. These days there is almost always something worth seeing in the capital, whether it is a remake of an old favourite or cutting-edge work from an emerging talent. Productions are usually of a very high standard.

![The splendid Victorian interior of the Olympia Theatre]

The splendid Victorian interior of the Olympia Theatre

INFORMATION SOURCES

Theatre listings can be found in *In Dublin* and the *Dublin Event Guide* magazines *(see p154)*. A monthly publication, *The Dubliner*, also has theatre reviews. Online resources include Entertainment (www.entertainment.ie), which also lists music and cinema venues and www.dublinks.com. Visit www.tickets.it to book tickets in advance.

MAINSTREAM THEATRE

The most famous venue is Ireland's national theatre, the **Abbey** *(see p70)*, which concentrates on new Irish productions, as well as revivals of Irish classics by playwrights such as Brendan Behan, Oscar Wilde, JM Synge and Sean O'Casey. The smaller **Peacock Theatre** downstairs runs more experimental work. Founded in 1928, the **Gate Theatre** *(see p72)* is still noted for its adventurous interpretations of well-known plays, while the highly regarded 1960s **Focus Theatre** produces plays from both new and established writers.

The **Gaiety** stages a mainstream mix of musicals, opera, ballet and plays, emphasizing the work of Irish playwrights.

With its Victorian music hall interior, the **Olympia Theatre** *(see p60)* stages comedy and popular drama. It is also well known as a music venue.

Other venues include the **Liberty Hall Theatre**, which offers an eclectic mix of drama, musicals and pantomime, and the **Tivoli Theatre**, which focuses on drama.

CONTEMPORARY/ AVANT-GARDE THEATRE

Some of the best fringe theatre in Dublin can be seen at the **Project** arts centre in Temple Bar. During the Dublin Fringe *(see Festivals)*, many other venues are also used, including Crawdaddy and The Sugar Club *(see p154 for both)* and art galleries.

The **Smock Alley Theatre**, dating from 1662, plays host to many dynamic theatre companies, including the acclaimed Rough Magic and Team Theatre.

The **New Theatre**, a small venue behind Connolly Bookshop, provides a mix of established and up-and-coming writers and directors, often with an Irish flavour.

New talent can also be found at university theatres. At the **Samuel Beckett Centre** at Trinity College, the standard is generally higher than you would expect from student theatre. **The Helix** at Dublin City University (DCU), near Glasnevin, has an excellent reputation for cutting-edge and diverse theatre and music. The **Teachers' Club** on Parnell Square is also a good spot to catch emerging talent. The **Axis** in Ballymun has a growing reputation for presenting work by emerging Irish playwrights.

Bewley's Café Theatre offers lunchtime performances of one-act plays or cabaret, usually by new writers, with a small cast. The shows cost €10 including lunch.

FESTIVALS

The **Dublin Theatre Festival** runs for two weeks between late September and early October, bringing together Irish and international talents to perform both new and classic works. An integral part of the festival is the Theatre Olympics, a programme of special events, forums, performances, exhibitions and workshops. Booking is highly recommended.

In mid-September, just ahead of the main theatre festival, is the **Dublin Fringe**, one of the country's largest contemporary performing arts festivals. The Fringe includes dance, street theatre, visual arts and comedy, with many performances taking place in the lush, mirrored Spiegeltent. Also in mid-September, puppeteers from across the world come to take part in the **International Puppet Festival**. The **Gay and Lesbian Theatre Festival** held

The Axis theatre in Ballymun

each year in May is a platform for both serious work and outrageous fun, while the vibrant **Festival of World Cultures** (late Aug) in Dún Laoghaire features theatre performances from all around the world, as well as music, art and circus.

A performance at the Dublin Theatre Festival

Diversions *(see p27)*, Ireland's largest and longest festival of free outdoor events, includes circus and drama performances.

Free tours of the Abbey and Gate theatres are included in **Culture Night**, one night in September when all cultural organizations open their doors to the general public. Visit www.templebar.ie for more details.

CHILDREN'S THEATRE

The Ark, a children's cultural centre in Temple Bar, has a packed programme of events, including drama. It is worth checking out, especially during the Dublin Theatre Festival. Around Christmas, the **Gaiety** *(see Mainstream Theatre)* and the **Olympia** *(see p60)* theatres attempt to outdo each other in lavishly produced pantomimes.

Eugene Lambert, a well loved puppeteer from Irish children's television in the 1980s, gives almost 30 performances a month in his famous **Lambert Puppet Theatre** and museum in Monkstown.

In mid-June, the Draíocht theatre company runs the annual **Spréacha Festival**, a six-day event of theatre, puppetry, storytelling and visual art for children aged between three and 12.

OUT OF TOWN

Outside of town are many more theatres that offer a mix of local amateur drama groups and professional touring companies. They include the **Pavilion** in Dún Laoghaire; **Draíocht** in Blanchardstown; the **Civic Theatre** in Tallaght; the **Millbank Theatre** in Rush; the **Mill Theatre** in Dundrum; and the Axis in Ballymun *(see Contemporary/Avant-Garde Theatre)*.

DIRECTORY

MAINSTREAM THEATRE

Focus Theatre
6 Pembroke Place.
Map E5.
Tel 676 3071.

Gaiety Theatre
King Street South.
Map D4.
Tel 677 1717.
www.gaietytheatre.ie

Liberty Hall Theatre
Eden Quay. **Map** E2.
Tel 872 1122.
www.centralticket
bureau.com

Tivoli Theatre
Francis Street.
Map B4.
Tel 454 4472.

CONTEMPORARY/ AVANT-GARDE THEATRE

Axis
Main Street, Ballymun.
Tel 883 2100.
www.axis-ballymun.ie

Bewley's Café Theatre
Grafton Street. **Map** D4.
Tel 086 878 4001.
www.bewleyscafe
theatre.com

The Helix
Collins Avenue, Dublin
City University, Glasnevin.
Tel 700 7000.
www.thehelix.ie

New Theatre
43 East Essex Street,
Temple Bar.
Map C3.
Tel 670 3361.
www.thenewtheatre.com

Project
39 East Essex Street.
Map C3.
Tel 881 9613/14.
www.project.ie

Samuel Beckett Centre
Trinity College.
Map E3.
Tel 896 2461.
www.tcd.ie/drama

Smock Alley Theatre
Essex Street.
Map C3.
Tel 679 9277.
www.gaietyschool.com/
smock_alley_theatre

Teachers' Club
36 Parnell Square West.
Map C1.
Tel 872 6944.

FESTIVALS

Dublin Fringe
Tel 679 2320.
www.fringefest.com

Dublin Theatre Festival
44 East Essex Street.
Map C3.
Tel 677 8439.
www.dublintheatre
festival.com

Festival of World Cultures
Dún Laoghaire.
Tel 230 1035.
www.festivalofworld
cultures.com

Gay and Lesbian Theatre Festival
179 South Circular Road.
www.gaytheatre.ie

International Puppet Festival
Tel 280 0974.

CHILDREN'S THEATRE

The Ark
11a Eustace Street.
Map C3.
Tel 670 7788.
www.ark.ie

Lambert Puppet Theatre
Clifton Lane, Monkstown.
Tel 280 0974.
www.lambertpuppet
theatre.com

Spréacha Festival
Draíocht, Blanchardstown.
Tel 885 2622.
www.draiocht.ie

OUT OF TOWN

Civic Theatre
The Square, Tallaght,
Dublin 24.
Tel 462 7477.
www.civictheatre.ie

Draíocht
Blanchardstown,
Dublin 15. *Tel 885 2622.*
www.draiocht.ie

Millbank Theatre
Chapel Green,
Rush, Co. Dublin.
Tel 843 7475.
www.millbanktheatre.
com

Mill Theatre
Dundrum.
Tel 296 9340.
www.milltheatre.com

Pavilion
Marine Rd, Dún Laoghaire.
Tel 231 2929.
www.paviliontheatre.ie

Outdoor Activities

The city of Dublin is only minutes away from open countryside, and Ireland has many activities to tempt all lovers of the outdoors. The beautiful Wicklow Mountains are within easy reach for scenic walks, and the coastline from Dublin Bay to Dun Laoghaire offers a range of sports including sailing, fishing and windsurfing. There are plenty of opportunities to go horse riding and cycling in the Dublin area. Entire holidays can be based around outdoor activities. In addition to the contacts on page 161, Fáilte Ireland and Dublin Tourism *(see pp164–5)* have information on all sports and recreational activities in and around the city.

Backpackers walking in the Dublin area

Fishing in the canal at Robertstown, County Kildare

FISHING

The claim that Ireland is a paradise for anglers is no exaggeration. Coarse, game and sea fishing all enjoy widespread popularity. Coastal rivers yield the famous Irish salmon, and, among other game fish, sea trout and brown trout also offer a real challenge.

Flounder, whiting, mullet, bass and coalfish tempt the sea angler; deep-sea excursions chase abundant supplies of dogfish, shark, skate and ling. You can organize sea-angling trips from many places.

Maps and information on fishing locations are provided by the **Central Fisheries Board** and the **Irish Federation of Sea Anglers**.

CYCLING

Cycling is very popular both in central Dublin and the countryside. If you prefer to bring your own bike, you can transport it fairly cheaply by train or bus. If not, you can always rent one from **Cycleways** or **Belfield Bike Shop** on the campus of University College Dublin. Also based here, **Irish Cycling Safaris** concentrate on trips outside Dublin, so you can enjoy the quiet country roads. The paths along Dublin Bay offer fun routes, while the Wicklow Mountains are more of a challenge. They also offer guided cycling tours of the city centre for groups.

The beautiful gardens of Powerscourt House *(see pp114–15)*

WALKING

Walking in Ireland puts you in the very midst of some glorious countryside. The network of waymarked trails takes you to some of the loveliest areas, inaccessible by car. Information on long-distance walks is available from Fáilte Ireland. Routes include the Wicklow Way, which leads from the south of Dublin into the heart of the beautiful Wicklow Mountains *(see p113)*. All the walks may be split into shorter sections for less experienced walkers or those short of time.

Hill walking, rock climbing and mountaineering holidays are also available in Ireland. For specialized information, contact the **Mountaineering Council of Ireland**. When walking or climbing always make sure that you go well-equipped for the notoriously changeable Irish weather.

HORSE RIDING AND PONY TREKKING

A number of riding centres, both residential and non-residential, offer trail riding and trekking along woodland trails, deserted beaches, country lanes and mountain routes. **Equestrian Holidays Ireland** organizes holidays for riders of various abilities. There are two types of trail riding – post-to-post and based. Post-to-post trails follow a series of routes with accommodation in a different place each night. Based trail rides follow different routes in one area and you stay at the same place for the whole holiday. Lessons are available at many riding centres for beginners to more advanced riders. Fáilte Ireland publish details of riding centres and courses.

Horseriding in Phoenix Park

WATER SPORTS

With a coastline of over 4,800 km (3,000 miles), it is small wonder that water sports are among Ireland's favourite recreational activities. Surfing, windsurfing, water-skiing, scuba-diving and canoeing are the most popular, and there are facilities for all of these along the Dublin coast and in Dublin Bay itself

Windsurfing is a popular sport throughout Ireland and there are a number of clubs and schools operating around Dublin Bay. **Surfdock** at Grand Canal Dock Yard and **Wind & Wave** in Monkstown both offer advice, tuition and the latest equipment.

There is a wide range of diving conditions off the coast of Ireland and the **Irish Underwater Council** will give you details of courses and their facilities.

Dun Laoghaire harbour at dusk

CRUISING AND SAILING

A tranquil cruising holiday is an ideal alternative to the stress and strain of driving, and Ireland's many rivers and lakes offer a huge variety of conditions for those who want a waterborne holiday. Stopping over at waterside towns and villages puts you in touch with the Irish on their home ground. Hiring a boat and drifting down the Grand Canal (*see p85*) from Dublin to the Shannon gives a unique view of the countryside.

Another popular sailing area is the scenic Howth peninsula, and the harbour of Dun Laoghaire southeast of Dublin, where you will find sailing schools offering tuition at all levels. For details of these schools, contact the **Irish Sailing Association**.

SPORTS FOR THE DISABLED

Sports enthusiasts with a disability can obtain details of facilities for the disabled from the **Irish Wheelchair Association**. Central and local tourist boards, and many of the organizations listed in the directory under each sport, will be able to offer facilities for disabled visitors. To be sure of this, it is advisable to call the venue first to check what is available.

Cycling in the Irish countryside

DIRECTORY

WALKING

Mountaineering Council of Ireland
House of Sport, 13 Joyce Way, Parkwest Business Park, Dublin 12.
Tel 625 1115.
www.mountaineering.ie

HORSE RIDING

Association of Irish Riding Establishments
11 Moore Park, Newbridge, Co Kildare.
Tel 045 431584.
www.aire.ie

Equestrian Holidays Ireland
www.ehi.ie

FISHING

Central Fisheries Board
Swords Business Campus, Co Dublin.
Tel 884 2600.
www.cfb.ie

Irish Federation of Sea Anglers
Mr Hugh O'Rorke, 67 Windsor Drive, Monkstown, Co Dublin.
Tel 280 6873.
www.ifsa.ie

CYCLING

Cycleways
185–186 Parnell St, Dublin 1. **Tel** 873 4748.
www.cycleways.com

Irish Cycling Safaris Belfield Bike Shop,
University College Dublin, Dublin 4. **Tel** 260 0749.
www.cyclingsafaris.com

WATER SPORTS

Irish Underwater Council
78a Patrick St, Dun Laoghaire, Co Dublin.
Tel 284 4601.
www.cft.ie

Surfdock Windsurfing
Grand Canal Dockyard, South Dock Rd, Ringsend, Dublin 4.
Tel 668 3945.
www.surfdock.ie

Wind & Wave
16a The Crescent, Monkstown, Co Dublin.
Tel 284 4177.
www.windandwave.ie

SAILING

Irish Sailing Association
3 Park Rd, Dun Laoghaire, Co Dublin.
Tel 280 0239.
www.sailing.ie

SPORTS FOR THE DISABLED

Irish Wheelchair Association
Áras Chúchulain, Blackheath Drive, Clontarf, Dublin 3.
Tel 818 6400.
www.iwa.ie

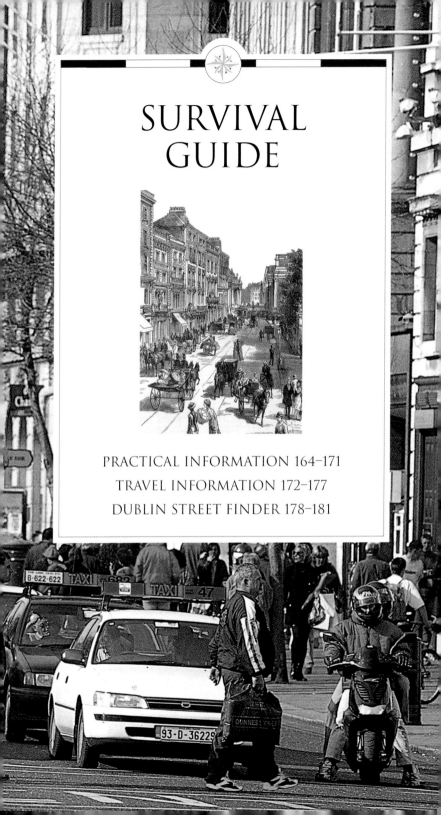

SURVIVAL
GUIDE

PRACTICAL INFORMATION

In the past few years, Dublin has enjoyed a dramatic renaissance. The renovation of the vibrant Temple Bar area, combined with the city's numerous museums, galleries and shops, attracts visitors in their thousands all year round. The best time to visit the region is probably late spring, before the peak summer season. Dublin is generally a safe place, but it does have a wide mixture of districts. You can very quickly find

Dublin Tourism logo

yourself out of a tourist area and in a less desirable part of town. It is wise to avoid the rougher areas to the north of the Liffey, away from O'Connell Street, especially at night. Transport around the city is good and taxis are readily available in the town centre. Dublin Tourism has geared itself up to the increasing demands of the tourist, and their office (in a converted church) is well organized with helpful and friendly staff.

Sign showing the way to Ardgillan Demesne

VISAS

Visitors from the EU, US, Canada, Australia and New Zealand require a valid passport but not a visa for entry into Ireland. All others, including those wanting to study or work, should check with their local embassy first. UK nationals do not strictly need a passport to enter Ireland but should take it with them for identification.

TOURIST INFORMATION

The tourist board for Ireland is **Tourism Ireland**, incorporating Fáilte Ireland and the Northern Ireland Tourist Board. Its network of overseas offices offer brochures and information.

Dublin Tourism is the regional authority for the Dublin area. The main office is in a converted church on Suffolk Street. There are also walk-in information offices at 14 Upper O'Connell Street, Baggot Street and Dublin Airport. Tourist offices sell maps and guide books, provide local information and can arrange car rental and reserve

accommodation. Their accommodation lists include only hotels and guesthouses approved by the tourist board. Museums and libraries often stock useful tourist literature.

ADMISSION CHARGES

Some of Dublin's major sights have an admission fee but many are free. For each place of interest in this guide, we specify whether or not there is a charge. Entrance fees are usually between 1 and 10 euros with discounts for students and the elderly. **The Heritage Service** maintains Ireland's parks, museums, monuments and gardens and issues a Heritage Card which allows unlimited access to more than 70 sites for a year.

Heritage card giving access to historic sites

Students at Trinity College, Dublin

STUDENT INFORMATION

Students with a valid ISIC card (International Student Identity Card) benefit from numerous travel discounts as well as reduced admission to museums and concerts. Buy a Travelsave stamp from any branch of **USIT** and affix it to your ISIC card to get a discount on various rail and bus services operated by Iarnród Éireann and Dublin Bus. You can also get a Temple Bar Culture stamp for discounts on cultural attractions in the area. ISIC cards can be obtained easily from any branch of USIT in Dublin.

USIT will also supply non-students under 26 with an EYC or IYC (European or International Youth Card) for discounts on airfares, and in restaurants, shops and theatres.

DUTY-FREE GOODS

In 1999 the duty-free allowances on goods bought by adults travelling between the Republic of Ireland and other countries were abolished.

However, a wide range of items may still be purchased at airport shops and on ferries, including goods that were previously duty-free, such as beers, wines, spirits, perfume and cigarettes. These shops can also be a useful source of souvenirs and last-minute gifts.

◁ **The main thoroughfare of O'Connell Street**

A selection of Ireland's quality daily newspapers

RELIGIOUS SERVICES

The Republic is 95 per cent Roman Catholic. For many people, churchgoing is a way of life; however, attendance is on the decline. Tourist offices, hotels and B&Bs keep lists of church service times.

IRISH TIME

The whole of Ireland is in the same time zone as Great Britain; five hours ahead of New York and Toronto, one hour behind Germany and France, and ten hours behind Sydney. Clocks go forward one hour for summer time.

NEWSPAPERS AND MAGAZINES

The Republic of Ireland has six national daily papers and five Sunday papers. Quality dailies include the *Irish Independent*, the *Examiner* and *The Irish Times*. The broadsheets are useful for information on theatre and concerts. Ireland's daily tabloid is the *Star*.

British tabloids are on sale throughout Dublin. Broadsheets such as *The Times* are also available. Local papers give details of what is on where, and when.

OPENING TIMES

Increasing numbers of shops are now open on Sunday afternoons. Some museums are shut on Monday. Opening hours are generally between 10am and 5pm but phone to check before your visit.

METRICATION

This has been taking place for a few years. Although most road signs are shown in kilometres, speed limits are still displayed in miles. Fuel is sold in litres, but beer is still sold in pints.

RADIO AND TELEVISION

Ireland has four TV channels, RTE 1, RTE 2, TV3 and TG4, which is an Irish-language service. There are six national radio stations and many local ones. The five British television channels can also be picked up in most parts of Ireland. Cable and satellite TV is quite common and is offered by most hotels.

FACILITIES FOR THE DISABLED

Most sights in Ireland have access for wheelchairs. However it is always worth phoning to check details. The Access Department of the **National Disability Association** provide useful information on amenities.

DIRECTORY

TOURIST INFORMATION

In Ireland
Tel 1850 230 330 (information).
Tel 1800 363 626 (reservations).
www.ireland.ie

In the UK
Tel 0800 039 7000 (info).
www.tourismireland.com

In the USA and Canada
Tel 1800 223 6470 (info).
Tel 1800 398 4376 (res).
www.tourismireland.com

EMBASSIES AND CONSULATES

Australia
Fitzwilton House, Wilton Terrace, Dublin 2. *Tel* 664 5300.
www.australianembassy.ie

Canada
65–68 St Stephen's Green, Dublin 2. *Tel* 417 4100.
www.canada.ie

UK
29 Merrion Rd, Dublin 4.
Tel 205 3700.
www.britishembassy.ie

United States
42 Elgin Rd, Ballsbridge, Dublin 4. *Tel* 668 7122.
www.usembassy.gov

USEFUL ADDRESSES

Dublin Tourism Centre
Suffolk St, Dublin 2.
Tel 605 7700.
www.visitdublin.com

The Heritage Service
6 Upper Ely Place, Dublin 2.
Tel 647 3000 or 1890 321421.
www.heritageireland.ie

National Disability Association
25 Clyde Rd, Ballsbridge, Dublin 4. *Tel* 608 0400.
www.nda.ie

USIT
19–21 Aston Quay, Dublin 2.
Tel 602 1904. www.usit.ie

LANGUAGE

The Republic of Ireland is officially bilingual – almost all road signs have names in English and Irish. English is spoken everywhere except for a few parts of the far west, an area known as the Gaeltacht, but now and then you may find signs only in Irish. On the right are some of the words you are most likely to come across when travelling around the Republic.

Sign using old form of Gaelic

USEFUL WORDS

an banc – **bank**
an lár – **town centre**
an trá – **beach**
ar aghaidh – **straight on**
bealach amach – **exit**
bealach isteach – **entrance**
dúnta – **closed**
fáilte – **welcome**
fir – **men**
gardaí – **police**
leithreas – **toilet**
mná – **women**
oifig an phoist – **post office**
oscailte – **open**
óstán – **hotel**
siopa – **shop**
sláinte! – **cheers!**
stop/stad – **stop**
ticéad – **ticket**
traein – **train**

Personal Security and Health

Although crime in Ireland has long been a relative rarity, in recent years bag-snatching, pickpocketing and car break-ins have become more and more prevalent on the streets of Dublin. Levels of crime are still low by international standards, but Dublin is a modern city with most of the accompanying problems, and visitors should not allow the fabled Irish friendliness to lull them into complacency. Tourist offices and hoteliers will gladly point out the areas to be avoided, but anyone who takes simple precautions should enjoy a trouble-free stay.

Police motorcyclist patrolling the busy Dublin streets

Garda station situated on Pearse Street, near the centre of Dublin

PERSONAL SECURITY

The police in Dublin and the rest of the Republic, should you ever need them, are called the **Gardaí**. Until recently, street crime was very rare in Dublin but, because of poverty and a degree of heroin addiction in certain areas of the city, it is now on a steady increase. However, if you use common sense when wandering around, there should be little cause for concern: avoid the backstreets or poorly lit areas at night; don't draw attention to yourself by wearing flashy jewellery; sit near the driver on buses; use a bag that can be held securely; be alert in crowded places.

You may be approached in the street by people asking for money. This rarely develops into a troublesome situation, but it is still best to avoid eye contact and leave the scene as quickly as possible. In

Light outside Garda station

general, safety in the city is about being alert to your surroundings. If you feel uncomfortable anywhere, especially at night, walk away confidently and head for well-lit, populated areas.

PERSONAL PROPERTY

Before you leave home, make sure your possessions are insured, as it can be expensive and difficult to do so in Ireland. Travel insurance for the UK will not cover you in the Republic, so ensure your policy is adequate.

As pickpocketing and petty theft can be a problem in Dublin, it is best not to carry your passport, air tickets or large amounts of cash around with you, or even leave them in your room. Most hotels have a safe and it makes sense to take advantage of this facility. Visitors carrying large amounts of money around should use traveller's cheques rather than cash *(see p168–9)*. When sitting in pubs and restaurants, keep your bag on your lap, if possible, and don't leave your wallet lying on the table. A money belt that can be worn under clothing is a good investment, as is a shoulder bag that can be carried across the chest with the opening facing inwards. When withdrawing money from cash machines, put the notes away as quickly as possible; don't stand around counting them.

Also, if there is a cash machine inside the bank, use that one in preference to one in the street.

If travelling by car, ensure that all valuables are out of sight and the car is locked, even when leaving it for just a few minutes. When you arrive at a hotel, ask the receptionist about secure parking in the area and, on trips out of Dublin to other towns, use guarded parking areas rather than street parking.

LOST PROPERTY

Report all lost or stolen items at once to the police. To make an insurance claim, you will need to get a copy of the police report. Most rail and bus stations in Dublin and the surrounding towns operate a lost property service.

Male and female Garda officers in ordinary uniform

Communications

eircom phone booth

Eircom is the republic's national telephone company. Although it no longer has the monopoly on the telephone services in the country, the majority of the city's telephone booths are still controlled by eircom. Their modern, efficient service includes coin, card and credit card telephones, distinguished by the wording around the top of each phone booth. Eircom phonecards are available from newsagents, post offices, supermarkets and other retail outlets.

Another company, Smart Telecom, also provides coin and credit card phones. Calls on their phones cost the same as those on eircom phones and are charged at a fixed rate of approximately 40c for 2 minutes.

MAKING A PHONE CALL FROM DUBLIN

Cheap rate calls within the Republic and to the UK are from 6pm to 8am weekdays and all day at weekends. Off-peak times for international calls vary from country to country, but are generally as above. Calls from hotels are expensive at all times.
• To make a call within the Dublin area, dial the seven-digit number, dropping the general Dublin area code 01.
• To make a call to an area outside Dublin, dial the area code which begins with a 0 and then the local number.
• To call Northern Ireland, dial 048, then the area code, followed by the number.
• To call other countries, dial 00, followed by the country code (for example, 44 for the UK), the area code (minus the leading 0), then the number.

USING AN EIRCOM PHONE

1 Lift the receiver and wait for the dial tone.

2 Insert your phone card into the slot or deposit any of the following coins: 10c, 20c, 50c, €1 or €2. The minimum amount is 30c. Dial the number and wait to be connected.

3 The display indicates how much credit you have left. A rapid bleeping noise means your credit has run out. Insert more coins or another card.

4 If you want to make a further call and you have credit left, do not replace the receiver, press the follow-on-call button instead.

5 To redial the number you have just called, press the button marked "R".

6 After you have replaced the receiver, retrieve your card or collect your change. Only wholly unused coins are refunded.

eircom phone card, available in various amounts

ACCESSING THE INTERNET

Dublin, like most major cities, has plenty of public access to computers and the Internet. Public facilities are available for free from libraries, but you may have to book in advance. One way to access the Internet is at one of the many Internet cafés found all over Dublin and throughout the country in major towns and cities. The cafés generally charge by the hour or half-hour for computer use, so costs build up quickly. Internet access is often cheaper during off-peak times. Bear in mind that UK-style three-pronged plugs are used in Ireland; adaptors may be needed.

Coffee and computers at the Central Cyber Café

TRAVEL INFORMATION

As Dublin becomes an increasingly popular tourist destination, the city becomes even easier to get to, with extremely frequent flights from the UK and good connections from elsewhere in the world. Ferry services are an alternative method of travel from the UK, docking at Dun Laoghaire harbour or Dublin Port. From both the airport and the harbours it is a short ride by car or bus into central Dublin. If you are planning to stay in the centre, it is not necessary to rent a car – most of the sights are within easy walking distance of one another, and the roads in the city centre can become very congested, particularly O'Connell Street. Should your feet require a rest, the bus services are frequent, and there are plenty of taxis available.

Aer Lingus Airbus in flight

The modern exterior of Dublin International Airport

FLYING TO DUBLIN

Flights from most of the main cities in Europe arrive at **Dublin Airport**, which is the Republic of Ireland's busiest airport. Regular services to Dublin depart from all five of the London airports (Heathrow, City, Gatwick, Luton and Stansted) and from 15 other cities in Britain, such as Leeds and Manchester, as well as the Isle of Man and the Channel Islands.

The major airline operating scheduled flights from Britain to Dublin is Ireland's national airline **Aer Lingus**. However since deregulation, their low-cost rival **Ryanair** has grown fast, with cheap fares from several airports in Britain and around Europe. From the United States, Aer Lingus and **Delta Air Lines** fly direct to Dublin Airport. However, there are no direct flights to Dublin from Australia and

New Zealand, so popular connecting points used by travellers include London, Singapore and Amsterdam.

AIR FARES

Airlines offer a host of options on air fares to Ireland from Britain. Usually, the amount you pay is determined by how flexible you are prepared to be and how far in advance you book your flight. The best bargains tend to be on flights for which the dates are not changeable. Flights from the United States can double in price in the summer and around Christmas when the fares are most expensive. Mid-week flights are often cheaper than weekend ones. The cheapest place to fly from in the UK is usually London, although the low-cost airline Ryanair flies from other locations in the UK and occasionally has very competitive

Airport sign in English and Gaelic

Shops
Bar
Snacks

deals. Ticket prices from the UK are generally fairly consistent throughout the year except at Christmas and during the summer when there are comparatively few discounted fares available. During these periods, due to the increased demand by visiting friends and relatives – usually referred to by airline companies as "VFR" – seats are taken well in advance so it is advisable to book as early as possible if you are intending to travel at these times. Many airlines offer discounts to those under 25, while USIT *(see p164)* and other agencies specializing in student travel often have cheaper rates for students and under-26s.

GETTING TO AND FROM THE AIRPORT

An express service, the Airlink bus, runs between Dublin Airport and the city's main rail and bus stations, from early morning to midnight. Tickets are purchased on board. A cheaper alternative are the number 16A and 41 city buses, which run to the city centre. Also, an efficient DART and bus connection runs via Howth Junction. Ask at your DART station for details. There is a taxi stand outside the airport and car rental companies inside. If you are flying from Dublin and wish to leave your car there or are collecting someone, there are long- and short-stay parking facilities.

The frequent-running Airlink bus

Irish Ferries ship loading up in the harbour

FERRIES TO DUBLIN AND DUN LAOGHAIRE

There is a good choice of ferry services from Wales to Ireland. **Irish Ferries**, the country's largest shipping company, sails on the Holyhead-Dublin route and has two crossings a day on the conventional ferry, which takes about 3¼ hours to reach Dublin Port. They also operate the Jonathan Swift high-speed service, which takes 1 hour 49 minutes. Irish Ferries does not operate on Christmas Day and St Stephen's Day (26 Dec).

The service from Holyhead to the south Dublin suburb of Dun Laoghaire – traditionally the busiest port in Ireland – is served by **Stena Line**'s Stena HSS (High-speed Sea Service). The HSS has the same passenger and vehicle capacity as conventional ferries but its jet-engine propulsion gives it twice the speed, cutting journey times in half. Vehicle loading and unloading times on the Stena HSS are also

shorter than on other ferries – the loading time for cars is about 20 minutes as opposed to a minimum of 30 minutes with most other ferries. Passengers requiring special assistance at ports or on board the ship should contact the company they are booked with at least 24 hours before the departure time. Like most other ferry companies, Irish Ferries and Stena Line take bicycles for a charge, and this should be mentioned when you make a reservation. The fast ferries may not run in rough weather. Stena Line's conventional ferries run from Dublin Port.

The **Isle of Man Steam Packet Company** operates the SeaCat Rapide service once a day between Liverpool and Dublin. The crossing takes four hours. Their Isle of Man crossing takes two hours, forty-five minutes.

PORT CONNECTIONS

All of Ireland's ports have adequate bus and train connections. At Dublin Port, available buses (with an extra fare) take ferry passengers into the city centre. From Dun Laoghaire, DART trains run into Dublin every 10 to 15 minutes, calling at Pearse Street, Tara Street and Connolly stations. These depart from the railway station near the main passenger concourse. Buses also run from outside Dun Laoghaire DART station to the city centre every 10 to 15 minutes. At all ports, taxis are readily available to meet arriving passengers.

Directions for ferry passengers

USEFUL NUMBERS

Dublin Airport
Tel 814 1111.
www.dublin-airport.com

Aer Lingus
Tel 0818 365 000 or 886 8844.
Tel 0845 084 4444 (UK).
www.aerlingus.com

British Airways
Tel 1890 626747.
Tel 0870 850 9850 (UK).
Tel 1800 403 0882 (US).
www.ba.com

British Midland
Tel 407 3036.
Tel 01332 854000 (UK).
www.flybmi.com

Cityjet
Tel 870 0300.
Tel 0345 445588 (UK).
www.airfrance.com

Delta Air Lines
Tel 1800 768080.
Tel 0800 414767 (UK).
Tel 1800 221 1212
or 1800 241 4141 (US).
www.delta.com

KLM
Tel 08705 074074 (UK).
Tel 1800 447 4747 (US).
www.klm.com

Manx Airlines
Tel 260 1588.
Tel 08457 256256 (UK).
www.manx-airlines.com

Qantas
Tel 407 3278.
Tel 02 6913636 (Australia).
www.qantas.com.au

Ryanair
Tel 0818 303030 or 609 7800.
Tel 0871 246 0000 (UK).
www.ryanair.com

Isle of Man Steam Packet Company
Tel 1800 805055.
Tel 01624 661661 (Isle of Man).
www.seacat.co.uk

Irish Ferries
Tel 1890 313131 or 661 0715.
Tel 08705 171717 (UK).
www.irishferries.com

Stena Line
Tel 204 7777.
Tel 08705 707070 (UK).
www.stenaline.ie

Stena HSS on the Dun Laoghaire to Holyhead crossing

Getting Around Dublin

Dublin is a fairly easy city to get around. The centre is relatively compact, so most of the sights are within walking distance of one another, and much of it, particularly south of the Liffey, is pedestrianized. If you are travelling into the city centre there is an excellent bus service and the local DART railway runs an efficient, if crowded, service to three city centre stations. The Luas line links the north and south of the city, the main railway stations and the centre to the suburbs. If you prefer to be driven around, taxis are available but are fairly expensive.

Parliament Street viewed from City Hall

Passengers boarding a Dublin Bus near Trinity College

GETTING AROUND BY BUS

Dublin Bus runs all the bus services in central Dublin and the Greater Dublin area. Bus stops for Dublin Bus are blue or yellow, and the numbers on them indicate which buses stop there. Buses in the city centre run approximately every 10 to 20 minutes from about 6am until 11:30pm, but do allow plenty of time if you have an appointment as they can run late. There is also a night bus service called Nitelink, which departs every hour from 12:30am to 2am Mon to Wed, 12:30am to 4.30am Thurs to Sat. If you are using the bus two or

three times in a day, it is worth getting a one-day pass, costing around 5 euros. There are also four-day, weekly and monthly passes. The main bus station is **Busáras** in Store Street, a short walk from O'Connell Street. You can catch the buses operated by **Bus Éireann** from here to destinations all over the country.

DART SERVICE

The convenient local electric rail service in Dublin known as the **DART** (Dublin Area Rapid Transit) serves 30 stations between Malahide in County Dublin and Greystones in County Wicklow with several stops in Dublin city centre. A Three Day Bus and Rail ticket costs 15 euros and allows three consecutive days' travel on DART trains and also covers Dublin Bus and local suburban rail. A Day Rambler ticket covers the same methods of transport but just for one day and costs around 8 euros. Family tickets for two adults and up to four children under the age of 16 are very good value. Tickets can be perchased at any of the DART stations.
Major works have

Logo on Bus Éireann local and express buses

been carried out along the DART line, including extensions northwards to Malahide and southwards to Greystones. There are some spectacular views along the southern section, particularly at Killiney and from Bray to Greystones.
The DART is very crowded and to be avoided at peak times during the week. The rush hours are between 7am and 9am and 5pm and 7pm.

LUAS

Luas, the Irish word for speed, is the new on-street light rail network, the first stage of which was completed in June 2004. The network will provide an easy and convenient way to reach areas of the city and the suburbs previously only connected to the city centre by bus. The first phase of the project saw the completion of two new tram lines. One runs west from Connolly Station along the north side of the Liffey. It then heads south at Heuston and terminates further south and west at Tallaght. The other line starts at St Stephen's Green and runs south to Sandyford. The **Luas** lines will eventually intersect with the DART and proposed Metro line, providing Dublin with an efficient and comprehensive transport system.

DART station sign

TAXIS IN DUBLIN

In Dublin, cruising taxis are around but the best places to find cabs are at taxi stands, hotels and rail or bus stations. Prices are based on metered mileage and the minimum charge is around 4 euros. There are a whole range of taxi companies in the city. If you want any information about taxis, the **Irish Taxi Federation** is happy to supply details and information about taxi companies.

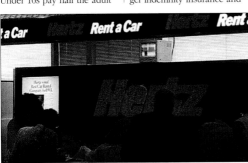

Taxis lined up outside the arrivals building at Dublin Airport

FARES AND TICKETS

In the Republic, long-distance buses are about half the price of the equivalent rail journey. If you are making the return trip on the same day, ask for a day-return ticket, which is much cheaper than the normal return fare. Also, between Monday and Thursday you can buy a "mid-week" return ticket for the price of a single journey. Under 16s pay half the adult fare. Students with a Travel-save stamp *(see p164)* get a 30 per cent reduction. For those intending to do a lot of travelling it is cheaper to buy a "Rambler" ticket. This allows unlimited bus travel throughout the Republic for a certain number of days in a set period, for example, 15 days' travel out of 30 consecutive days.

The distinctively marked Dublin City Tour bus

BUS TOURS

Bus Éireann and some local companies run half- and one-day excursions in Dublin. Dublin Bus (Bus Átha Cliath) runs the Dublin City Tour, which leaves from O'Connell Street Upper and takes in the city's most famous sights, including St Stephen's Green, the Bank of Ireland and the Parliament as well as some more obscure sights, such as Oscar Wilde's home. The witty commentary alone makes the tour well worth doing.

DRIVING

If you do not take your own car, there are plenty of car rental firms to choose from. Car rental can be expensive in peak season and the best rates are often obtained by booking in advance. Broker companies, such as **Holiday Autos**, use the major rental companies and will shop around to get the best deal. Car rental usually includes unlimited mileage plus passenger indemnity insurance and cover for third party, fire and theft, but not vehicle damage.

To rent a car, you must show a full driver's licence, which you have held for two years without violations. Cars are usually rented only to those aged between 23 and 70, but some companies may make exceptions. For a list of suggested car rental companies in Dublin see page 177.

PARKING

Dublin has "pay and display" areas, parking meters and car parks. Parking on the street is allowed, although a single yellow line along the edge of the road means there are some restrictions (there should be a sign nearby with permitted parking times). Double yellow lines indicate no parking at any time.

Disc parking – a version of "pay and display" – also operates in Dublin. Discs can be bought from local newsagents, petrol (gas) stations, tourist offices and many small shops.

DIRECTORY

USEFUL CONTACTS

Bus Éireann
Tel 836 6111.
www.buseireann.ie

DART & Irish Rail
Tel 836 6222. www.irishrail.ie

Dublin Bus Information
Tel 873 4222.
www.dublinbus.ie

Holiday Autos
Tel 872 9366.
www.holidayautos.co.uk

Irish Taxi Federation
Tel 836 4166 or 855 1487.

Luas
Tel 1800 300 604. www.luas.ie

A busy Hertz car rental desk at Dublin Airport

Travelling Outside Dublin

One of the best ways to see the magnificent scenery in the countryside around Dublin is by car. The roads have improved greatly in the last few years but the number of cars has also increased. One of the quickest ways to get to more distant destinations is by train. Ireland's national rail network is fast and efficient and also provides an ideal way to see the country's dramatic landscape. Alternatively, you can enjoy the countryside at your own pace by touring on a bicycle, although a certain degree of fitness is advisable if you are going to tackle the beautiful Wicklow Mountains.

Rural petrol pump

Purchasing a rail ticket at a station ticket office

TRAIN SERVICES IN IRELAND

The two main rail stations in Dublin are Connolly, for trains to the north, northwest and Rosslare; and Heuston, which serves the west, midlands and southwest. These two stations are connected by the red Luas and the No. 90 bus service, which runs every 10 to 15 minutes and takes a quarter of an hour, but can take about 30 minutes at rush hour. Irish Rail (Iarnród Éireann) operates a service out of Dublin to most large cities and towns. Going by rail is probably the fastest and most convenient way of

travelling to other major places. Most trains have standard and super-standard (first-class) compartments. Bicycles can be taken on trains for a supplement of around 10 euros.

TICKETS AND FARES

Throughout Ireland, train tickets are generally quite expensive, but there are lots of good-value incentive or concessionary passes. Most of these include bus travel, so you can travel to virtually anywhere in Ireland on just one ticket.

The most comprehensive ticket available, the Emerald Card, can be used on Irish Rail, Dublin Bus and Bus Éireann services. For around 180 euros it gives eight days' unlimited travel in a 15-day period. An 8-day Irish Explorer ticket is slightly cheaper and is valid on all Irish Rail and Bus Éireann transport. The Irish Rover ticket can also be good value. It is valid on all rail and bus journeys from three days within an 8-day period. For

15 euros students can buy a National Student Travelcard for a discount on all Irish Rail single and return journeys, as well as on DART and Dublin Bus services. Older travellers can get InterRail Plus 26 cards costing 7 euros.

DRIVING YOUR OWN CAR

If you intend to use your own car, check your insurance to find out how well you are covered. To prevent a comprehensive policy being downgraded to third-party cover, ask your insurance company for a Green Card. Carry your insurance certificate, Green Card, proof of ownership of the car and, importantly, your driver's licence. If your licence was issued in the UK, bring your passport for identification.

Membership of a reputable breakdown service is advisable unless you are undaunted by the prospect of breaking down in remote countryside. Non-members can join up for the duration of their holiday only. Depending on the type of cover you have, breakdown organizations may offer only limited services in Ireland so check before you travel.

If you are renting a car, make sure the insurance cover meets your needs. You will need to show your driver's licence – if you are a US citizen you will need an International Driving Permit, available from the **AAA**.

GÉILL SLÍ

Yield (give way) road sign in Gaelic

Platform of Heuston Station in Dublin

RULES OF THE ROAD

Even for those unused to driving on the left, driving in Ireland is unlikely to pose any great problems. For many visitors, the most difficult aspect of driving on Ireland's roads is getting accustomed to passing other vehicles on the right and giving way to traffic on the right at round-abouts. The wearing of safety belts is compulsory for drivers and for all passengers whether they are sitting in the front or rear seats. All children must be secured with a suitable restraint system. Motorcyclists and their passengers are obliged by law to wear crash helmets.

View of Dun Laoghaire from the road around Killiney Hill *(see p91)*

Junction ahead   **Unprotected quay or river ahead**

Dangerous bends ahead   **Children or school ahead**

ROAD SIGNS

Most road signs in Ireland are in both Gaelic and English. Most are also now in kilometres although some signs may still appear in miles. The sign "Yield" is the same as the UK "Give Way". Brown signs with white lettering indicate places of historic or cultural interest.

BUYING FUEL

Unleaded fuel and diesel fuel are available just about everywhere in Ireland. Although prices vary, fuel is relatively cheap by European standards. Almost all the petrol (gas) stations accept VISA and MasterCard, though check before filling up, particularly in rural areas.

SPEED LIMITS

The maximum speed limits in Ireland, which are shown in miles, are more or less the same as those in Britain:
• 30 mph (50 km/h) in built-up areas.
• 60 mph (95 km/h) outside built-up areas.
• 70 mph (110 km/h) on highways.
On certain roads, which are marked, the speed limits are 40 mph (65 km/h) or 50 mph (80 km/h). Where there is no indication, the speed limit is 60 mph (95 km/h). Vehicles towing caravans (trailers) must not exceed 55 mph (90 km/h) on any road.

CYCLING

The quiet roads of Ireland help to make touring by bicycle a real joy. **Belfield Bike Shop** and **Cycleways** are good rental outlets in Dublin. If you are venturing further afield, local tourist offices will give you details of bike rental in their area. You can often rent a bike in one town and drop

Road signs in the Republic in Gaelic and English

it off at another for a small charge, or put it on the train. Many dealers also provide safety helmets, but bring your own waterproof clothing to help cope with the weather.

DIRECTORY

CAR HIRE COMPANIES

Argus Rent-a-Car
Tel *490 4444.*
www.argusrentals.com

Avis
Tel *1890 405060.*
www.avisworldwide.com

Budget
Tel *844 5150.*
www.budgetcarrental.ie

Dan Dooley
Tel *677 2723.*
www.dan-dooley.ie

Hertz
Tel *844 5466.*
www.hertz.ie

Murrays Europcar
Tel *812 0410.*
www.europcar.ie

BREAKDOWN/ INSURANCE SERVICES

American Automobile Association (AAA)
www.aaa.com

Automobile Association
Tel *1800 667 788 (freephone).*
www.aaireland.ie

Royal Automobile Club
Tel *1800 535 005 (freephone).*
www.rac.ie

BICYCLE-HIRE SHOPS

Belfield Bike Shop
Tel *716 1697.*

Cycleways
Tel *873 4748.*

Street Finder Index

KEY TO THE STREET FINDER

▪ Major sight	🚍 Coach station	✝ Church
▪ Place of interest	🚕 Taxi rank	⊠ Post office
▪ Railway station	🅿 Main car park	═ Railway line
🄳 DART station	ℹ Tourist information office	– One-way street
🚊 Luas stop	✚ Hospital with casualty unit	▬ Pedestrian street
🚌 Main bus stop	👮 Police station	

0 metres 200
0 yards 200
1:11,500

KEY TO STREET FINDER ABBREVIATIONS

Ave	Avenue	**E**	East	**Pde**	Parade	**Sth**	South
Br	Bridge	**La**	Lane	**Pl**	Place	**Tce**	Terrace
Cl	Close	**Lr**	Lower	**Rd**	Road	**Up**	Upper
Ct	Court	**Nth**	North	**St**	Street/Saint	**W**	West

General Index